THE SURPRISING SIDE OF GRACE

Discovery House PUBLISHERS

BOX 3566 · GRAND RAPIDS. MI 49501

*PUBLISHING BOOKS THAT FEED
THE SOUL WITH THE WORD OF GOD.*

THE SURPRISING SIDE OF GRACE

Appreciating
God's
Loving Anger

STEPHEN A. BLY

The Surprising Side of Grace
Copyright © 1994 by Stephen A. Bly

Unless otherwise indicated, Scripture is taken from the
Holy Bible, New International Version.
Copyright © 1973, 1978, 1984 International Bible Society.
Used by permission of Zondervan Bible Publishers.

Library of Congress Cataloging-in-Publication Data

Bly, Stephen A., 1944–
     The surprising side of grace : appreciating God's loving anger /
Stephen A. Bly.
          p.   cm.
     Rev. ed. of : God's angry side. c1982.
     ISBN 0-929239-89-X
     1. God—Wrath. 2. Conduct of life.   I. Bly, Stephen A., 1944–
God's angry side. II. Title.
BT153.W7B56   1994
231.7—dc20   94–11149
                                                          CIP

Discovery House Publishers is affiliated with Radio Bible Class,
Grand Rapids, Michigan 49512

Discovery House books are distributed to the trade by
Thomas Nelson Publishers, Nashville, Tennessee 37214

Printed in the United States of America

94 95 96 97 98 99 / CHG / 10 9 8 7 6 5 4 3 2 1

For a list of other books by Stephen A. Bly, or for information
regarding speaking engagements, write:

Stephen A. Bly
Winchester, Idaho 83555

Table of Contents

For
Bill Crowder
a good partner . . .
on the trail

Chapter 1

The Least Explored
Side of God's Character

I love Jesus and Janet.

And Russell, Michael, Aaron, Lois, Michelle, Zachary, and Miranda, to name just a few.

We can learn a lot about a person by the ones and the things he loves. Most often, this is the first thing we learn about a newcomer.

I also love riding horseback in the Rockies, watching sunsets on the Sonoran desert, attending rodeos in Cheyenne, watching the breakers at Rio Del Mar, and enjoying T-bone steaks cooked medium-rare.

I love books by J. I. Packer, music by the Sons of the San Joaquin, art by Charles M. Russell, sculpture by Frederic Remington, pickup trucks by GMC, rifles by Winchester, novels by William Saroyan, and fishing in the Florida Keys.

I love praying by myself on an empty mountainside in Nevada, reading the Bible before daylight, preaching to standing-room-only crowds, and baptizing new believers.

The list could go on and on.

But if we really want to know a person, if we desire to get the entire picture of what one is like, we will want to dig deeper. At some point in the relationship we will want to find out the things one hates. What makes one angry? Even in a world of weak and sinful people, we learn much about a person's character by exploring the things one dislikes.

I never buy anything from telephone solicitors. In fact, I prefer not to talk to them—ever.

I get upset when folks fail to be prompt for meetings and appointments.

I get defensive when people compliment me in order to manipulate my behavior.

I come close to furious when I see a child or a woman being physically mistreated.

It takes intense self-control to keep me from confronting aggressively a person who slanders or ridicules Jesus.

I don't think you know me well until you know the things that make me angry—and why.

Now, the same is true about God.

When we first come to knowledge of Him we are most often overwhelmed by His love. And we should be.

Paul prays that we "may have power, together with all the saints, to grasp how wide and long and high and deep is the love of Christ" (Ephesians 3:18).

God's love is unparalleled and unmeasurable

1. God's love, from the beginning, has been a central part of His plan for us.

"In love he predestined us to be adopted as his sons through Jesus Christ, in accordance with his pleasure and will" (Ephesians 1:4–5).

2. It is a global love intended for those of every tribe and tongue.

"For God so loved the world that he gave his one and only Son, that whoever believes in him shall not perish but have eternal life" (John 3:16).

3. God's love is personal, with each one of us experiencing that love much the same as Paul did when he said: "The life I live in the body, I live by faith in the Son of God, who loved me and gave himself for me" (Galatians 2:20).

4. It is a love that brings us salvation.

"Because of his great love for us, God, who is rich in mercy, made us alive with Christ even when we were dead in transgressions—it is by grace you have been saved" (Ephesians 2:4–5).

5. It is God's love that brings us into His family.

"How great is the love the Father has lavished on us, that we should be called children of God! And that is what we are!" (1 John 3:1).

6. God's love comes with objective proof.

"God demonstrates his own love for us in this: While we were still sinners, Christ died for us" (Romans 5:8).

7. It is a love that continually encourages us.

"Hope does not disappoint us, because God has poured out his love into our hearts by the Holy Spirit, whom he has given us" (Romans 5:5).

8. God's love never fades, nor will it be ripped away from us.

"I am convinced that neither death nor life, neither angels nor demons, neither the present nor the future, nor any powers, neither height nor depth, nor anything else in all creation, will be able to separate us from the love of God that is in Christ Jesus our Lord" (Romans 8:38–39).

And these verses are just the first light of God's great love for us. When we realize that the Creator and Sustainer of all that exists knows every last sinful detail and motive of our lives and yet sent His Son to be our Savior, we should be astonished. Basking in that love, we accept Christ as our personal Lord and Savior, are filled with His Holy Spirit, and push on to live a holy and righteous life in cheerful obedience to His Word.

God's love is meant to be read, studied, accepted, and experienced. We should feel very loved by God.

But, like all of those we love, there will be a time in our Christian life when we begin to wonder, *Have I made God angry? Does He really get angry at all?*

The Surprising Side of Grace

What about God's anger? When was the last time you studied the subject? When was the last time you heard a sermon or Bible study on this theme?

Christian maturity means growth in knowledge of God.

Paul reveals a glimpse of what this maturity looks like when he states, "We pray this in order that you may live a life worthy of the Lord and may please him in every way: bearing fruit in every good work, growing in the knowledge of God" (Colossians 1:10).

Jeremiah lets us peek into the heart of God when he states, " 'Let not the wise man boast of his wisdom or the strong man boast of his strength or the rich man boast of his riches, but let him who boasts boast about this: that he understands and knows me, that I am the LORD, who exercises kindness, justice and righteousness on earth, for in these I delight,' declares the LORD" (Jeremiah 9:23–24).

Anyone desiring to truly grow in knowledge of God will want to come face-to-face with understanding His anger. Even a superficial review of a concordance will show that there are as many references in the Bible to God's anger, fury, and wrath as there are to His love.

This does not, of course, mean that we serve an angry God. We serve, rather, a loving God who does, at times, get angry. This is, perhaps, the least explored side of His mercy and grace. It is like the back side of a mountain that many climbers never bother exploring. To appreciate God's loving anger is to understand the surprising side of His grace.

God's anger is His just, intense indignation and displeasure caused by the injury, insult, injustice, and wickedness of mankind, both individual and corporate. J. I. Packer calls it "a right and necessary reaction to objective moral evil" (*Knowing God,* J. I. Packer, InterVarsity Press, Downers Grove, IL, 1973, page 136).

But God's anger continues to be a subject that most of us would like to avoid. Sometimes we feel it's a dark, foreboding, secretive, threatening topic. Maybe it should be reserved for the theologians and their research papers. Or we imply that maybe it should be studied only after all other biblical themes are mastered.

Postponing such a study doesn't follow the biblical pattern. John MacArthur, Jr., states, "The gospel is not all good news. In fact, it is not good news at all for those who turn away from Christ. Note that the starting point for Paul's gospel is God's wrath against sin: 'For the wrath of God is revealed from heaven against all ungodliness and unrighteousness of men" (Romans 1:18). Paul then spends more than two full chapters systematically proving that all humanity is sinful and under the wrath of God" (*Ashamed of the Gospel,* John F. MacArthur, Jr., Crossway, Wheaton, IL, 1993, page 131).

Excuses We All Use to Avoid Considering God's Anger

1. If God is a God who gets angry, He may be angry with me.

Melissa went to a Bible college about 1,200 miles from home. It was her first experience in a big city, making her own choices and setting her own schedule. At first she dated a different guy every weekend. But after a while she settled down to Scott. By their last year at Bible college they were married.

Now they live in a little town in Oklahoma, where Scott owns a farm implement dealership. Melissa's been married eight years, has three children, and has had, by her own admission, a half-dozen affairs with men in the community. She goes to worship every Sunday, Bible study on Thursdays, and often sings solos in church. She confessed Jesus as Lord and Savior years ago and believes that God hasn't given up on her.

Her fourth pregnancy ended in a miscarriage and now she is wondering, *Is God angry with me? Is this His way of punishing me?*

11

But she refuses to study the subject of God's anger. She's hoping maybe God just loves everyone, no matter what they do. She doesn't want to find out if He's angry with her, because she knows He has every right to be.

2. When I get angry, it's because I've lost control of myself. Therefore, God cannot get angry because He's always in control.

Jack's a neighbor, and a pretty nice fellow. He's an excellent mechanic, and if you have a problem with your rig, he always seems to show up at the front door with toolbox in hand ready to help.

But he does have a dangerous flaw. Jack likes alcohol. Likes it so much that most Friday nights find him unmanageably drunk. And when Jack is drunk he is angry and violent; the kids get slapped, his wife punched, and the neighbors cursed.

The next morning, when he regains control, he is shocked by his behavior and is sincerely apologetic. In Jack's mind, anger is a destructive demon that torments his loved ones, and himself.

It's hard to talk to Jack about God's anger. "What kind of God is He if He gets mad all the time?" he protests. "I just don't think God is that way. He loves us—even old drunkards like me."

Jack's right to think that God does not get angry in the same way we do. Another chapter is devoted to that theme. But he's critically wrong to think God never gets angry.

3. If I discover that God is angry with me, I will be forced to change my thoughts and/or behavior, which I do not want to do.

Right after he got married, Jared found a job in sales. He was delighted to find out that he loved the work, and he was very good at it. In those early years he told his wife, Linda, that he would work Sundays only until he gained seniority enough to have another day off. "In a couple of years I'll get back to going to church with you."

But that was many years and several children ago and Jared still works Sundays. He claims he can't give it up now; it's his best day of the week for sales. "Man, I make enough on Sundays to cover the mortgage payment on the cabin at the lake plus the boat payment combined!"

Jared has no interest in learning anything about God's anger. "What if I find out He's angry with me for working Sundays? That would be a bummer, now, wouldn't it? Maybe I'm better off just being dumb."

4. To talk about an angry God will repel people from the salvation Christ has to offer. I want those around me to be attracted to Christ, not turned off by a negative message.

I received a call from Stella Matthews about 9:00 on a Monday morning. "Pastor? Would it be possible for you to put the theme of next week's sermon in the bulletin each week?" I apologized to her admitting that I just don't always know the exact theme that far in advance.

"Well, don't get me wrong," she continued. "I enjoyed yesterday's sermon about God's anger. However, if I had known the subject, I certainly wouldn't have brought the Flanigans."

"The Flanigans?" I asked.

"Our new neighbors. I've been looking forward to bringing them with us. They seem to be having some marriage problems. And this being the third go-round for each of them, they certainly didn't need to hear about the Lord's anger," she protested. "I'll never get them back to church now!"

But I believe that if the Flanigans come face-to-face with the real nature of God, they'll be back every week.

5. If I discover that I have incurred God's anger by my thoughts or actions, it will greatly depress me, causing sorrow and grief. I'd rather avoid the subject and thereby avoid the ensuing depression.

Traci wears pink.

Lots of pink.

Pink boots, pink jeans, pink blouses, pink lipstick, pink earrings, and a pink hat. She drives—you guessed it—a pink Jeep.

She says, "Pink makes me happy!" And it seems to be her goal in life to always be happy. She's the volunteer adviser to the cheerleaders at the high school, organizes the big community Fourth of July show, and is in charge of delivering Christmas cookies from the church to shut-ins during the holidays.

She finds the book of Philippians delightful, Galatians depressing, and some of the Psalms "positively horrid! They're so depressing. I just know the Lord wants us all to be happy!"

Traci's never provided a chapter and verse to back up her theology. But one thing's for sure—she doesn't want to talk about God's anger.

"The world's depressing enough," she complains, "without talking about God getting mad!"

God's Anger Examined

I write western novels.

The sorrel horses gallop, the Colt .44s blaze, and good always triumphs over evil. To make them realistic I am constantly reading historical accounts of the Old West. I've got about ten bookshelves crammed with volumes on history of the Old West, and I'm needing to build more.

A friend called me up the other day and asked what I could tell him about Shoshone Chief Washakie's role in the big peace treaty of 1851, southeast of Ft. Laramie.

Actually, I didn't even know Washakie was there. I had thought that the Shoshones were excluded from that particular council. I immediately dug through some books and studied up on the subject. It's the kind of thing I should have known.

What do you and I really know about God's anger?

If we're members of His family it's exactly the kind of thing we should know. And if you stand outside a personal relationship with God, then a study of His anger will definitely challenge your position.

Here are three reasons I believe we must study God's anger.

1. A warped view of another's character destroys a relationship.

Jim's fairly new to our area. I knew him a few years back when we both lived in another state. He always struck me as a rather negative sort of guy, always finding fault with those around him.

He stopped by the other day and told me about a run-in he'd had with a neighborhood restaurant owner named Reynolds. "He's the most unethical cheat I've ever met," Jim exploded. "And I told him so!"

Now, the truth is, I've known Kelsy Reynolds for several years and always found him to be a generous man who gives of his time, talent, and money to meet the needs of others. I can't remember when he refused a meal to a drifter. Nor can I think of any community cause that he didn't fully support.

Jim can call Reynolds any name he wants, but it just doesn't stick. I know what the man is truly like. Of course, I don't suppose I'll ever get Jim to change his mind. If we persist in holding on to our own personal, inaccurate view of another we'll never really get to know him or her at all.

In the same manner you and I can assign any extrabiblical qualities we like to God. We can say He's 6'4", gray-haired, muscular, and has a pencil-thin mustache. We can say He's kindly, slightly forgetful, and walks with a cane.

Or we can delete any character traits we don't want Him to have. We can eliminate His fury, judgment, wrath, and anger.

You see, we can add traits or subtract them. Either way, it will weaken, if not destroy, our relationship with Him.

We will be associating with our own image of God, not who He really is. And no relationship based on misrepresentation can be very deep or strong.

Does God really get angry?

Yep.

How often does this happen?

Listen to what the Scriptures say, "God is a righteous judge, a God who expresses his wrath every day" (Psalm 7:11).

That doesn't mean that He gets mad at you and me every day. But it does mean that the objective moral evil in our lives and in our world continually provokes His right and necessary reaction to it.

Until we are ready to accept that and understand what that means to us personally, our relationship to Him will never be as complete as it could be.

2. Because ignoring the subject could actually increase God's anger.

Paul reminds us to "consider . . . the kindness and sternness of God" (Romans 11:22).

God's anger, in the life of a believer, is always remedial. It is meant to bring about a solution, to cure a moral or spiritual problem. If His slight displeasure fails to bring about the proper resolution, perhaps His full-fledged expression of anger will catch our attention.

In Zechariah 1:15 the Lord says to the prophet, "I am very angry with the nations that feel secure. I was only a little angry, but they added to the calamity."

Ignoring the desired effect of God's anger adds to the misfortune of individual people like you and me, as well as nations.

3. Because creating God in a self-decided image is idolatry.

16

If our god never gets angry then we're worshiping some other god, it's not the God of the Bible. This practice is condemned as idolatry.

"You shall have no other gods before me" (Exodus 20:3)—not the gods that other religions have created—nor the ones you and I conjure up.

"Be careful to do everything I have said to you. Do not invoke the names of other gods; do not let them be heard on your lips" (Exodus 23:13). This wrong image of God should not occupy our minds or our lips for even a moment.

"They exchanged the truth of God for a lie, and worshiped and served created things rather than the Creator—who is forever praised. Amen" (Romans 1:25). In having a god who is never angry, we would be throwing away God's truth and holding on to a lie.

"Therefore, my dear friends, flee from idolatry" (1 Corinthians 10:14). How serious is this problem of holding on to the wrong picture of God's character? It's so serious we should run from it as we would from a wild animal about to devour us.

All of that should motivate each of us to push on and study the subject of God's just and righteous anger.

But it probably won't.

If we had our choice, we'd rather follow the dangling carrot than be pushed by the crack of a whip. So, what will all this study bring to you and me? Where's the benefit?

We will discover exalted respect for God's character.

We will learn what kinds of things are so precious to Him, that to reject them stirs his anger. We will learn that His anger is not like ours at all. We will find a compassionate, patient, kind heavenly Father who, nonetheless, refuses to put up with our rebellion.

We will discover greater confidence in His protection.

A parent who never gets angry poses a hazard to a child. The neighborhood bully can come into his home

17

and beat him up, and the parents will do nothing. The school can give his hard-earned grades to another student, and the parents will say nothing. His brother who's 100 pounds bigger can constantly steal his supper, and the brother never has to face the fury of the parents' anger. Such a relationship would be frightening as well as bizarre.

Sometimes we assume God is sort of that way. The psalmist had a brief bout with doubt when he said, "This is what the wicked are like—always carefree, they increase in wealth. Surely in vain have I kept my heart pure; in vain have I washed my hands in innocence" (Psalm 73:12–13). To the writer, there was a moment when he forgot about God's anger. And without that, the world seemed so unjust and holiness so pointless.

But clarity of thought came to him when he remembered God's anger. It was in the sanctuary where he considered the whole nature of God's character. "Surely you place them on slippery ground; you cast them down to ruin. How suddenly are they destroyed, completely swept away by terrors! As a dream when one awakes, so when you arise, O Lord, you will despise them as fantasies" (Psalm 73:18–20).

Our heavenly Father will show His just anger, and we can count on His righteous protection.

We will discover increased motivation for holiness and obedience.

If idolatry, for instance, angers God, then true worship is extremely important to him. I will want to enthusiastically release myself to that worship. If a broken vow angers God, then integrity has meaning, and I will more faithfully attempt to keep every promise. If denying Christ as my personal Lord and Savior draws God's wrath, then I will make my confession plain and clear to all those around me.

It is not merely to avoid God's wrath that I will obey. But it is, rather, that God's wrath reveals how important some things are to Him. And if I love Him, I will desire to do those things He deems important, not for fear of punishment but out of a desire to show love.

We will discover deeper trust in God's design for this world.

In a way, God's anger is proof that He has a plan for this world—and for my life. If God were willing to let civilization take any old turn it wanted, then He would just sit back and watch us progress like a child watching a spinning top slow down. But His anger comes to individuals and nations as they begin to spin out of His plan.

His anger reminds us that history (both personal and corporate) is not arbitrary. Through Zechariah the prophet, the Lord instructs, "Whoever touches you touches the apple of his eye" (Zechariah 2:8). Try to thwart God's plan for Israel, for instance, and you will get an immediate taste of His anger (just as you instantly react when someone pokes your eyeball).

God's a little touchy when it comes to trying to circumvent His blueprint for this old world. That brings great confidence for those of us who desire His will to be done.

We will discover a clearer understanding of the intensity of His love.

In another chapter we'll look at how God's anger differs from our own. There we will discover that God is not quick to anger nor does He let petty matters stir Him to wrath.

But when God does get angry, He demonstrates beyond all doubt what things are important to Him.

Phil and Angela sat across the desk from me in my office and began to pour out some of the problems they were facing in their marriage. It was Angela's turn and her disappointment turned to anger even as she spoke.

"Sure it's an eight-hour drive, but in fourteen years of marriage he never once took me and the kids to my folks' house for Thanksgiving!" she cried out.

The Surprising Side of Grace

Phil cleared his throat, swallowed deep, and sheepishly whispered, "I, eh, I never knew it meant that much to you. We'll go this year, I promise."

It was an interesting line. "I never knew it meant that much to you," he said. Not until Angela showed some anger. Then it dawned on him what he had overlooked for fourteen years.

You and I can overlook God's heart, too.

And just sometimes, it's His anger that wakes us up and reveals the intensity of His love.

What does God's anger look like?

Two hundred homes along the Pacific coast incinerate in a brush fire and are completely destroyed. Is this God's anger at work?

Tens of thousands of homosexuals are now infected with the HIV virus which leads to AIDS and death. Is this God's anger?

A local civic leader was caught in an affair with his neighbor's wife; now he has lung cancer. Is this God's anger?

Two teens were out drinking on a Friday night and plowed their rig into a tree. One is paralyzed for life. Is this God's anger?

You promised God last January that you would read the Bible every day, but you gave up by March. And now, it's July and you didn't get that big promotion at work you had been counting on. Is this God's anger?

Many times it's difficult for us to identify God's anger in the current events in our lives. And it's almost impossible to recognize God's anger toward another person.

We live in a fallen world. Many tragedies result from the natural consequences of living in a world that has been bent out of shape by the sin of humankind. The earth quakes, rivers rise, shots are fired at random, bridges collapse, airplanes crash—and none may be direct expressions of God's anger.

There's a better course than trying to look back and study God's anger as it might have looked in action against specific individuals or peoples. Instead, we'll study the difference between His anger and our own; then we'll be looking at the Scriptures to discover the specific kinds of things that activate His just anger now. That way, even though we can't always identify his anger in the past or present we will know how to avoid it in the future.

There will, of course, be some surprises along the way. An angerless God would be one who cared little whether His words were obeyed or His deeds honored. Such a God would be one who said nothing of importance and did little of significance. The Bible knows no such God.

Nor do we.

God love will never be ripped away Rom. 8:38-39

Living the Word

1. List five things that God loves (give biblical references). *God loves everyone - Eph. 1:4-5*
God loves a personal relationship - Gal. 2:20
God loves salvation Eph. 2:4-5
God loves to encourage us Romans 5:5

2. List five things that make God angry (give biblical references). *Idolatry - Exodus 23:13   Denying Christ*
That His Plan - Zech. 2:8
Broken vows -   Disobedience

3. What bothers/worries/frightens you most about studying the topic of God's anger?

That I will find He is angry with me.

4. Have you ever experienced God's anger? If so, describe the event.

5. Study the following Psalms: 2:4–5; 7:6; 27:9; 30:4–5; 56:7; 77:9; 78:38; 85:1–7; 90:7–9; and 145:8–12. Which of these passages most closely express your sentiments at the present time about God's anger?

derisive

6. Prayer: You might want to pray through Psalm 6:1–3:

> *O LORD, do not rebuke me in your anger or discipline me in your wrath. Be merciful to me, LORD, for I am faint; O LORD, heal me, for my bones are in agony. My soul is in anguish. How long, O LORD, how long?*

Chapter 2

It All Looks
Different From Above

Each of us is an artist.

We all paint pictures.

We dip into the wellsprings of shapes, sizes, colors, concepts, ideas, dreams, and experiences—and out of these we unfold intricate masterpieces of imagery in our minds. Imagination is a gift of God given at Creation. It enlivens potentially dull lives, breaks up boredom, and snaps us out of lethargy with its puissance for flashes of ingenuity.

Yet, at times, our imaginations fail us.

There are limits to what we can conceive.

Take the subject of God, for instance. Our minds strain to grasp an understanding of what He is like. The information fed into our computer-like brains does not all fit into our preset categories. God is too immense.

So we have a standoff between the vastness of God and our limited, meager minds. One possible solution would be to devise a way to raise our capacity for wisdom and knowledge. But we have so far to go. It seems hopeless. "The foolishness of God is wiser than man's wisdom, and the weakness of God is stronger than man's strength" (1 Corinthians 1:25).

Even in the catapulting acceleration of scientific knowledge in our century, we are still at a loss when trying to define such things as time, space, energy, and eternity. Is it any wonder that we have trouble understanding all there is to know about the Lord God Almighty?

Since we can't boost our intelligence enough, we try to lower God to the reach of our understanding. We humanize Him. And we've been doing that for a long time. In theology the word is anthropomorphizing. Here's how it works.

Any beginning Bible reader knows that God is Spirit (John 4:24). Therefore He is not confined to a physical body as we know it. But it's hard for you and me to discuss a bodyless person in loving, intimate terms. So we anthropomorphize Him. Listen to how that sounds (italics added):

"Your *hands* made me and formed me; give me understanding to learn your commands" (Psalm 119:73).

"The *eyes* of the LORD are on the righteous and his *ears* are attentive to their cry; the *face* of the LORD is against those who do evil" (Psalm 34:15–16).

"The eternal God is your refuge, and underneath are the everlasting *arms*" (Deuteronomy 33:27).

Now we have a God who has hands, eyes, ears, arms, and a face. This helps us to relate to Him in a personal way.

We do the same thing with God's personality.

The Bible says God is wise. "To the only wise God be glory forever through Jesus Christ! Amen" (Romans 16:27). So we think of God as Grandpa Miller who knew the answers to every childhood question.

We are told that God is knowledgeable. "Lord, you know all things" (John 21:17). And we think of God as Professor MacMillen who had three doctorates and was fluent in twenty-six languages.

We learn that God is good. "Give thanks to the LORD, for he is good; his love endures forever" (Psalm 118:29). Which reminds of us Miss Torres who lived next door and never said an unkind word about anyone in her whole life.

We're taught that God is loving. "Whoever does not love does not know God, because God is love" (1 John 4:8). Which makes us think of Mom when we skinned our knee and she rocked us in her lap.

The Bible reveals that God is gracious. We are "justified freely by his grace through the redemption that came by Christ Jesus" (Romans 3:24). Which makes us think about our fourth grade teacher, Mrs. Welch, who let us turn in our History of California Missions report even though we accidentally dropped it in the mud on the way to school.

Then we discover that God is holy. "Who among the gods is like you, O LORD? Who is like you—majestic in holiness, awesome in glory, working wonders?" (Exodus 15:11). And holiness reminds us of Mr. Hannah who taught junior-high and high-school Sunday school for twenty-five years.

We read that God is truthful. "God is not a man, that he should lie, nor a son of man, that he should change his mind. Does he speak and then not act? Does he promise and not fulfill?" (Numbers 23:19). All of which reminds us of Mrs. Williams at the corner market who would always count our change out penny by penny and never let us pay too much.

We study the Bible and discover that God is just. "Righteousness and justice are the foundation of your throne; love and faithfulness go before you" (Psalm 89:14). And we imagine one like Judge Houk, sitting stately in the municipal court.

On and on the list could go. When we discover a quality about God we look for a similar quality in someone around us. Then we say to ourselves, "That's the way God is!" To a point that is a helpful process. We do need to make our relationship with God personal. He is not a blind force, an abstract energy field, or merely an ideal image of good.

The Surprising Side of Grace

But our mistake comes when we begin to think we can limit God to human categories. We are mistaken, for instance, if we learn what love is like from our relationship to our mate, and then project its ultimate expression to God. Instead, we should learn what love is like by getting to know God, and then apply that trait to ourselves and others.

It all looks so different from above.

And this is an extremely important distinction. God is not a glorified, sinless, exalted man. His character is uniquely His own and will not be contained in human categories.

A good example of this is when we take a look at God's anger. Our normal pattern is to think of a situation in which we have been angry—or when people have been angry with us—and then say to ourselves, "That's the way God's anger is."

But God's anger is not like ours.

There are at least four faults with our anger that are never a part of God's.

1. Our anger is capricious.

We are impulsive, unpredictable, and fickle.

In 1 Samuel 18–27 we have a picture of the relationship between King Saul and David. Saul, grateful for David's triumph over Goliath, showed him honor by bringing him into the royal household. Then Saul twice attempted to kill David by throwing a spear at him. Saul promised to give David his daughter Merab for a wife. He changed his mind and gave him Michal instead. Saul became afraid of David and chased him off. When Jonathan, Saul's son, interceded, Saul restored David to the household.

Saul once again threw a spear at David. He pursued David with his whole army, but David refused to harm Saul when he had opportunity. Saul, finding out about David's loyalty, repented for a while, then set out again to kill

26

David. Still, David refused to harm Saul when he had the opportunity, and again Saul repented and invited David to come home, but David refused.

Man's anger, as seen in Saul, is so unpredictable that we don't know what to expect next. "I wonder what kind of mood he'll be in today" we say of a boss, co-worker, or spouse. Sometimes moods erupt without apparent logic.

God is not that way.

He is not moody.

He does not have bad days.

2. Our anger is self-indulgent.

Human anger may be controlled by selfish desires. We use it as a weapon to get things for ourselves.

In 1 Kings 21 we see an account about Ahab, the king of Israel. It seems that he had a palace in the beautiful, fertile valley of Jezreel. A man named Naboth owned a small vineyard close to the palace. Gazing over the countryside one day, Ahab decided it would be nice to have a garden close by. Just a place to stroll through in the heat of the day and pluck a few figs or cucumbers. In fact, Naboth's vineyard would be a perfect place for the king's garden.

So Ahab offered to buy the vineyard, but Naboth declined. To sell was out of the question. That vineyard had been in the family since the days of Joshua. In response, Ahab stormed into his bedroom and refused to eat supper. He pouted in anger. Jezebel, Ahab's wife, consoled him by arranging Naboth's death and confiscating the property.

We react like Ahab in closer-to-home situations. We march out of the living room in a huff because the family would not agree to watch a particular television program. We yell at the kids because they used the sports page in the cat litter box before we had a chance to read it. We exchange harsh words with our wife because the "extra" money we had been saving for fishing gear was used to buy new bathroom curtains.

Our anger is often motivated by selfishness.

God's never is.

It is not self-indulgent.

3. Our anger is petty.

Most often, the matters over which we become angry are trivial.

It happens to even the best of disciples.

You remember James and his brother, John? They traveled with Jesus to Jerusalem passing through Samaria in what we might call the West Bank today. In those days many avoided going through that area because they feared spiritual pollution. Jesus didn't seem to worry about such things. While approaching a Samaritan village, He sent some of the disciples ahead to arrange for provisions. The Samaritans refused them.

James and John were shocked at the lack of hospitality. "Lord, do you want us to call fire down from heaven to destroy them?" (Luke 9:54). In the anger of the moment they felt that denial of a meal deserved annihilation of the whole city. "But Jesus turned and rebuked them" (Luke 9:55). The "Sons of Thunder" (Mark 3:17), as Jesus would call them, were way too trivial with their anger.

God's anger is never petty.

4. Our anger is touchy.

We're easily annoyed. Anger comes quickly. At times, we think of such a reaction as a strong, positive quality.

Take a look at Lamech in Genesis 4:19–24. He had been offended. A lad struck out in anger against Lamech and wounded him. So Lamech hit back. But he didn't return wound for wound. He killed the boy, and then bragged to his family. "No one can mess around with me and get away with it!" he said in effect.

We're sometimes that way. We use anger to force our way upon others.

God's anger is different.

He is not easily disturbed.

We will only begin to grasp the quality of God's anger when we can set aside our ideas that anger is always capricious, self-indulgent, petty, and touchy. His anger stems from a pure and loving heart that will not and indeed cannot harbor an evil motive.

Seven things to remember about God's anger

1. God's anger is always justified.

With regard to God's anger, no one has a legitimate right to say, "But, Lord, it isn't fair!"

God is always fair. His anger always has a just cause.

When we cry out to God that He is being unfair, we assert that we are not receiving what we deserve. But think that through. Do you and I really want to receive all that we deserve? *good point*

The Bible reminds us that there is a direct relationship between our actions and God's reaction. "You, O LORD, are loving. Surely you will reward each person according to what he has done" (Psalm 62:12). That's what we call justice. Only the mature are able to accept reproof and correction without resentment.

Never, ever has a person faced the wrath of God without just cause.

Robert complained because he got custody of his two daughters only one weekend per month. "It's not fair! Why is God doing this to me?" He should have considered all that before he ran off to Las Vegas for a week with that young waitress.

God is not a divine referee who sometimes makes bad calls. His anger is always justified.

2. God's anger is always initiated by disobedience.

There would be no occasion for divine anger in a sinless world. Adam and Eve, wandering through the trees before the Fall, never once witnessed God's anger. He did warn them that they would be punished if they chose to disobey. But they must not have believed Him.

29

They soon learned the truth—and tasted of His anger.

In Genesis 4 there is the familiar account of Cain and his brother, Abel. God "did not look with favor" on Cain's offering (4:5). God saw into Cain's heart. He warned him to persevere in his struggle against sin. But Cain became even more rebellious. Rather than master the sin, he allowed it to master him. He killed his brother. God's anger and his punishment was just. Cain complained that it wasn't fair. "My punishment is more than I can bear" (4:13). But he was wrong. God is fair. Cain did survive . . . east of Eden.

Paul quotes Malachi when he says, "Jacob I loved, but Esau I hated" (Romans 9:13). Why did God hate Esau? Was it just an act of divine arbitrary selection?

Nope.

Esau, the eldest, thought lightly of the promises of God. The Lord God may have promised a great nation and many future blessings to his grandfather Abraham and father, Isaac, but Esau lived only for the present. "What do I get out of it right now?" he demanded to know.

Faith is believing that God has done, is doing, and will do all that He has said He will do. Esau demonstrated his lack of faith when he traded his birthright for a bowl of stew. Hebrews 12:15–17 explains the dilemma: "See to it that no one misses the grace of God and that no bitter root grows up to cause trouble and defile many. See that no one is sexually immoral, or is godless like Esau, who for a single meal sold his inheritance rights as the oldest son. Afterward, as you know, when he wanted to inherit this blessing he was rejected. He could bring about no change of mind, though he sought the blessing with tears."

God showed his anger toward Adam and Eve, toward Cain, toward Esau; but in every case it was their own actions that precipitated God's reaction. The amazing thing in each of these passages is not that God becomes angry. Surely each of us gives Him ample reason. The astounding thing is that God does not often show anger. He is a gracious, loving, forgiving, and merciful God.

His anger is based on our actions.

His mercy comes in spite of our actions and comes solely from the heart of a loving Father.

3. God is slow to anger.

"But you, O LORD, are a compassionate and gracious God, slow to anger, abounding in love and faithfulness" (Psalm 86:15).

Jonah knew this, but he didn't like it.

When God called him to preach to the Ninevites, Jonah did not want to go. They were a fierce and cruel people. They had devastated the land of Israel. As far as Jonah was concerned, they did not deserve to hear the words of the Lord.

So he fled from God's call. The great fish spit him out on the shore, and he reluctantly went to Nineveh. Walking throughout the city Jonah blasted them with doom: "Forty more days and Nineveh will be overturned" (Jonah 3:4).

His assignment completed, Jonah squatted on a hillside overlooking the city. He wanted a good view of the destruction. But it never came. The people believed Jonah and repented. They humbled themselves before God. So the Lord postponed their calamity. Jonah was furious. He was angry at God.

"O LORD, is this not what I said when I was still at home? That is why I was so quick to flee to Tarshish. I knew that you are a gracious and compassionate God, slow to anger and abounding in love" (Jonah 4:2).

When it comes to other people, we want God's anger to be instant and his retribution swift. That's what we would do if we were Him.

But we aren't Him.

And He isn't us.

When the evil of our word is not punished instantly it doesn't mean that God doesn't care. It doesn't mean that he is powerless. He sees, He remembers, He will insist on justice. But let us stand in awe of His patience, seeing how much He puts up with while He waits for us to recognize His love and change our ways. "The Lord is not slow in keeping his promise, as some understand slowness. He is patient with you, not wanting anyone to perish, but everyone to come to repentance" (2 Peter 3:9).

4. God's anger does not last long.

"Sing to the LORD, you saints of his; praise his holy name. For his anger lasts only a moment, but his favor lasts a lifetime; weeping may remain for a night, but rejoicing comes in the morning" (Psalm 30:4–5).

The exile of God's people that followed the destruction of Jerusalem in 587 B.C. was an expression of God's anger. What had they done to deserve such drastic action? Jeremiah 2:32 tells us: "My people have forgotten me, days without number." The Lord further declares, "My people are fools; they do not know me. They are senseless children; they have no understanding. They are skilled in doing evil; they know not how to do good" (Jeremiah 4:22). Their failure is summed up in Jeremiah 35:15: "You have not paid attention or listened to me."

Rampant apostasy. Perverted worship. Corrupt priests. The people rejected God's love and forgiveness. What did they deserve? Enslavement? Abandonment? Death?

Even as God allowed the temple to be destroyed and Jerusalem laid in ruins, even as the people were herded off to a foreign land, even then God promised to bring them back and show His compassion once again. According to Jeremiah's prophecy the punishment would take seventy years (Jeremiah 25:11–12). In the history of an individual man, that's a whole lifetime. In the history of this world, it's but a blink of the eye.

"His anger lasts only a moment" (Psalm 30:5). It's quite unlike yours and mine.

5. God often restrains His anger.

None of us has ever felt the full power of God's displeasure. When Adam and Eve rebelled, they claimed authority that belonged to God. He had forewarned them what the punishment would be. If He had struck them down immediately, that would have been just.

But He didn't do that.

He did herd them out of the Garden. They did experience a cessation of close fellowship with God as they had known it before. They were given plenty of time to think over what they had done. And He continued to watch over them.

The people of Israel felt God's fury many times. They faced plagues and pestilences and military defeats. But they never, ever faced the full wrath of God.

"He was merciful; he atoned for their iniquities and did not destroy them. Time after time he restrained his anger and did not stir up his full wrath" (Psalm 78:38).

Jesus, too, restrained His anger. In the account of the woman caught in adultery (John 8:1–11) the religious leaders were correct in assuming that she had committed a heinous offense against God. The Bible clearly condemns adultery. Jesus could have justly ordered the woman's (and the man's) death. But Jesus restrained His judgment.

Why?

Shouldn't every infringement on God's commands be quickly and thoroughly punished? Isaiah 48:9 gives us the answer, "For my own name's sake I delay my wrath; for the sake of my praise I hold back from you, so as not to cut you off."

If God did not restrain His anger, there would be no one left to praise Him, to bring Him glory. To catch a frightening glimpse of God's just anger coming to earth in full strength, re-read the book of Revelation. A glance at almost any chapter there will remind us that God's anger is greatly restrained in our present age.

6. God's anger is neutralized by our repentance.

Let's not try to fool ourselves. God is not a department-store Santa Claus, paid to tell us nice things. Remember Hebrews 10:31 warns that "it is a dreadful thing to fall into the hands of the living God." And Romans 11:22 reminds us, "Consider therefore the kindness and sternness of God: sternness to those who fell, but kindness to you, provided that you continue in his kindness."

Our rebellion against God should throw us into great fear and dread of the consequences of our actions.

David was a mighty king, a mighty warrior, and a mighty sinner. Nathan knew that only too well. In a burst of spiritual fortitude, Nathan confronted the powerful king about his sins of adultery and murder. David's instant response is noteworthy. "I have sinned against the LORD" (2 Samuel 12:13).

David didn't try to justify his actions by blaming them on the stress of his job. He didn't deny what he had done. He didn't even try to rationalize that the deeds were not so bad after all. He recognized sin as sin. He cast himself upon God's mercy. And Nathan replied, "The LORD has taken away your sin. You are not going to die" (2 Samuel 12:13). There would be painful consequences for David to bear, but he would be forgiven.

God longs to see people repent so He can shower forgiveness on them. But most folks are not like David. Most of us just cannot admit to a failure. We fear relinquishment of the control of our lives. Repentance conjures up concerns about loss of pleasure, success, or prestige.

David knew his only hope was to cast himself on the mercy of God. Another time when he sinned, he was given a choice of three punishments. He could either be handed over to men, to the furies of nature, or into the hands of the living God. "Let us fall into the hands of the LORD, for his mercy is great; but do not let me fall into the hands of men" (2 Samuel 24:14). It is better to leave your fate in the hands of an angry God than in the hands of angry people.

While repentance might be the hardest thing to do at the moment, it is always beneficial in the long run.

• Repentance involves our emotions. We must feel sorrow for our actions. "Blessed are those who mourn," Jesus says in Matthew 5:4. Many believe the meaning there to be, "Blessed are those who mourn and grieve over their sins."

• Repentance involves our minds. We must proclaim our guilt to God after serious thought. This is no time for excuses. Rationalizing wastes time. Sin is sin. And it is sin against God Himself.

• Repentance involves our will. We must decide to stop what we're doing and resolve to correct the fault. We can't underestimate the power of our own wills. They get us into horrible trouble, and they (with the Holy Spirit's help) can pull us out again.

• Repentance involves our bodies. Action is required. We have to absolutely stop doing something. And usually a positive action is required to replace it.

• Repentance involves our spirit. Receiving the gift of God's grace should evoke a response of praise and thanksgiving. True repentance requires the use of every aspect of our beings. God deserves nothing less.

7. God's anger remains until it accomplishes its purposes.

God's anger is not supposed to be the final state of our relationship with God. It has a function. It is a tool to achieve God's will.

"The anger of the LORD will not turn back until he fully accomplishes the purposes of his heart. In days to come you will understand it clearly" (Jeremiah 23:20).

God is not a moody, temperamental despot who will change His mind if we give Him some time. When God is angry, there is a problem that needs correction. His anger is not diminished until the situation is rectified.

Jonah fled from the will of God and ran up against His anger. The sea grew rough and the big fish snapped. But down in the fish's belly, Jonah repented. From that point on, Jonah's condition improved.

The Israelites wandered in the wilderness for forty years. When Caleb and Joshua were the only two adults left of the original escapees from Egypt, then, and only then, they entered the Promised Land. God's purpose in His anger had been accomplished.

Paul (at the time still called Saul) was blinded on his way to Damascus. Three days later, in an act of submission and humility before the very people he had come to arrest and imprison, Paul received his sight again. God's will had been done.

Many Christians believe in the heavenly permissive parent. They think that once they have joined God's family He will never be angry with them again. That works, provided we never rebel or disobey. When we fail to repent we find ourselves on the receiving end of God's anger and discipline.

It would be foolish to ignore the reality of God's anger. And it would be just as imprudent to think that His anger duplicates ours. God's anger is a tool for Him to use when we choose to ignore His grace, mercy, and love.

And God's anger will never fail to accomplish the purpose for which He intended it.

Living the Word

1. Can you remember the last five times you were angry? Jot down each instance. (If you can't remember, ask someone who knows you well to help out.)

a. At Dan when he put work ahead of meal time.
b. At our workers when they complain out a lot.
c. When customers do not pay bills + lie.
d.
e.

Now in each instance answer the following: What was the cause of my anger? At whom was I angry? How was the situation resolved? On a scale of one to ten, how important to the long view of my life, was this event?

After thinking these things through, how would you say God's anger differs from yours?

It is selfish!

2. Study Hebrews 12:7–11. If we are children of God, then when we provoke His just anger, we will probably also face His discipline. From this text name at least four benefits we will receive from His discipline.

- *Share in His Holiness – Peace*
- *Produces of Harvest of righteousness – Healing*

3. Complete this sentence: "The thing I appreciate most about God's anger is *it is for my good*." Why did you give this answer?

Because of the benefits of his anger bring about desirable qualities.

4. You might like to make Psalm 143:1–2 your prayer:

> O LORD, hear my prayer, listen to my cry for mercy; in your faithfulness and righteousness come to my relief. Do not bring your servant into judgment, for no one living is righteous before you.

Chapter 3

His Obvious Anger

God's Anger in the Old Testament

In our quest to know God better—by understanding and avoiding His loving anger—we will discover some actions that are simple to understand and ones that are obviously offensive to Him. These will naturally be ones that we have already purged from our lives. Or at least we hope so.

Take idolatry, for instance. Worship of any god other than the Lord God is prohibited in Scripture. The second commandment is clear: "You shall not make for yourself an idol in the form of anything in heaven above or on the earth beneath or in the waters below. You shall not bow down to them or worship them; for I, the LORD your God, am a jealous God, punishing the children for the sin of the fathers to the third and fourth generation of those who hate me, but showing love to a thousand generations of those who love me and keep my commandments" (Deuteronomy 5:8–10).

Now, it's understandable to most that such behavior brings out God's anger. If He is who He claims He is, then to worship another god is the chief of all insults. Primitive people had a problem with their statues and idols, but those of us born in the enlightened twentieth century have long set aside such uncivilized vices. Or have we?

Maybe we should take another look at idolatry. Suppose that nine thousand feet up the side of Mt. KeKautel, buried deep in one of the world's most rugged mountain ranges, is perched the tiny town of Xequa. About one hundred small adobe homes cling to the side of the mountain. A long, winding, windswept path about eighteen inches wide connects this village to the rest of the world below.

Progress is slow here. Cultural change is measured in centuries. A resident might not see any government workers for several months. It will be decades before they have such things as electricity or running water.

But that's just the way these fiercely independent natives want it. The only variation in their simple architecture is a huge raised platform in the center of the town square. Here sits Ke Ka, a thirteen-foot, gold-covered stone statue of a grotesque kneeling man with a face of an eagle who has four arms that all point to the peak of Mt. KeKautel. It is reported that once a month the people of Xequa assemble to sacrifice produce and livestock to their god. The elaborate ceremony includes many songs, chants, and pleadings for health and prosperity.

Rumors have filtered down the mountain that an occasional human sacrifice has been offered in tough times of famine or war.

Is this idolatry?

Inside Sylvia's living room is a treasured collection of religious statues and artifacts. Over the worn beige sofa is a large ceramic cross with a graphic plaster-of-paris portrayal of a crucified Jesus. On the coffee table is her pride and joy, a black marble likeness of Mary and the baby Jesus. Her hobby includes collecting pictures of Jesus. At last count twenty-five versions hung on the walls of her one-bedroom home.

She also has praying hands statues, a life-size Jesus holding a sheep, and even a statue of St. Peter. Sylvia claims she can remember God better with all these helps. The scented candle burning beside the black marble figures reminds her to pray for Tony, her husband, who died seven years ago. .

The Surprising Side of Grace

Is this idolatry?

Mabel McPherson teaches philosophy and basic moral issues at the local community college. She is a member of First Church of Stocton where Dr. Hampton preaches. This educated man has studied in Germany, Switzerland, and Scotland. He is always quoting the latest theologians, philosophers, and poets. Mabel has been influenced by Dr. Hampton's conclusion that Christianity is the most helpful of all the world religions.

She often asks her freshman philosophy students to define God. Mabel is continually amazed at their primitive, anthropomorphic concepts. She spends weeks during the course of the semester defining God as the Great Creative Principle, the Prime Cause of the universe. For her, thoughtful minds through the centuries have written down their experiences with this One. The Bible is one of the more ancient examples of such writing. Other classics (from Plato to Mary Baker Eddy) can be equally inspiring. She believes that Jesus probably was in tune with the Prime Cause better than any other man in history.

Mabel considers herself a very religious person.

Is this idolatry?

Wayne sits on the third pew of the Lakeside Bible Church every Sunday morning (except for the weekend elk-hunting season opens). He loves good Bible preaching and singing gospel songs. Wayne accepted Christ in that very same church at the age of twelve and has been active in its life and ministry ever since.

But Wayne doesn't spend much time with personal Bible study. He claims that he's on the road so much during the week he just doesn't have time. But he does listen daily to his favorite radio Bible teacher.

Three weeks ago Wayne got upset with his pastor. It seems that Brother Jamison spoke about the need to reach out into the remote areas of the earth to present Christ's saving gospel. "Why, if we don't go, who will? Are we going to

let those men, women, boys, and girls who've never heard of
Jesus, die and go to hell before they've had a chance to
repent?"

That's the line that ticked Wayne off the most. He just
knew that God would never condemn those who had
never heard the gospel. Although he could not think of a
verse to support his claim, he did know what God is like.
"After all," he complained to his wife, "I've been a Christian for almost thirty years. I just don't think God would do
a thing like that, no matter what the preacher says!"

Is this idolatry?

What about these four accounts? Are they all idolatry?
We could probably all agree on the first example. Bowing
down to the golden statue certainly looks like a clear case
of idolatry. But what about the Sylvia and her images? Or
Mabel and her redefinition of God? Or Wayne who
believes he knows exactly what God is like, regardless of
the biblical account.

Are they all forms of idolatry?

Absolutely.

Do they all stir up God's just anger?

Yep.

It seems that from the fall of mankind and the entry of
sin into the world we have been plagued with the worship
of false gods. It's no wonder, since as Genesis 6:5 reminds
us, "The LORD saw how great man's wickedness on the
earth had become, and that every inclination of the
thoughts of his heart was only evil all the time."

Centuries later, when the Ten Commandments came to
Moses and the people of Israel, idolatry was overt and rampant. It was a difficult commandment for the people of Israel
to keep. Temptations surrounded them. A partial listing of
the Middle-Eastern gods vying for their attention include:

In Egypt   Aten-Re, the sun god
                Amon-Re, king of the gods
                Khepera, the beetle god

Khensu, the moon god
Osiris, god of the dead
Isis, Osiris' wife, goddess of fertility
Horus, Osiris' son, the sky god

In Mesopotamia

Anu, god of the heavens
Istar, goddess of fertility
Enlil, god of the earth
Tammuz, god of the plants and vegetation

In the region of Palestine

Baal, the storm and vegetation god
Baalzebub, god of the flies
Asherah, Baal's consort
Dragon, chief god of the Philistines

From the time of the Exodus from Egypt until the return of the exiles from Babylon, the number one problem the Hebrew nation faced was idolatry. The good leaders and kings fought it. The bad ones gave in to it. Because of idolatry God says, "Do not follow other gods, the gods of the peoples around you; for the LORD your God, who is among you, is a jealous God and his anger will burn against you, and he will destroy you from the face of the land" (Deuteronomy 6:14–15).

Worship of man-made idols is a high offense against God. It is the most insulting and insidious of all sins. God alone deserves the worship, adoration, devotion, and honor of those He has created. But idolatry doesn't stop with bowing before a physical image. Idolatry involves dreaming up wrong mental images of God as well. J. I. Packer points out, "It needs to be said with the greatest possible emphasis that those who hold themselves free to think of God *as they like* are breaking the second commandment" (*Knowing God*, J. I. Packer, InterVarsity Press, Downers Grove, IL, 1973, page 42).

Thus idolatry, which seems at first glance only a primitive and ancient transgression, has a much broader definition and can still be found today. It might not be a gold statue, but rather a crystal hanging around the neck. The pressure to worship another god might not come from the village witch doctor with a shrunken head on his spear. It might come to us from two nicely dressed, polite young men in dark suits and ties who appear at our front door.

Idolatry exists in every age.

And in every instance it arouses God's just anger.

Yes, the villagers of Xequa are committing idolatry. But consider again Sylvia, Mabel, and Wayne?

Sylvia and her religious artwork would have a hard time avoiding the charge of idolatry. Let's assume that she doesn't think of any of those statues or pictures as actual gods. "I don't worship the artifacts," she explains, "but the God they represent."

But who is the God they represent?

"Sylvia, is God loving?"

"Why, certainly. Do you see what kind eyes he has in that black velveteen picture over the kitchen table?"

But Sylvia has never seen God. How does she know about His eyes?

"Sylvia, does God ever get angry?"

"Why, heavens, no! Look at that face," she points to the living room picture of Jesus who floats above the path by the door. "I don't think a person like that could get angry with anyone."

Attributes of God are defined for Sylvia in her religious artifacts and her pictures of Jesus.

Now, the Scriptures tell us God is indeed loving. But that is based on the Word of God, not out of the mind of an artist or sculptor. What if the artist was wrong in his interpretation of God? Then all who accept this as a proper representation will be led to follow a false god.

The Bible presents other views of Jesus that can give us glimpses of God. In fact, Jesus said, "Anyone who has seen me has seen the Father" (John 14:9). So in Revelation 19 we get this picture: "I saw heaven standing open and there before me was a white horse, whose rider is called Faithful and True. With justice he judges and makes war. His eyes are like blazing fire, and on his head are many crowns. He is dressed in a robe dipped in blood, and his name is the Word of God. Out of his mouth comes a sharp sword with which to strike down the nations. 'He will rule them with an iron scepter.' He treads the winepress of the fury of the wrath of God Almighty" (19:11–15).

Sylvia doesn't have any pictures of this view of God. She believes in a sort of selective misrepresentation, which could lead her into idolatry.

Remember Mabel? She believes in God, the Prime Cause. Her view stems largely from a nineteenth-century deistic approach (the subject of her master's thesis). The "Biblonians," as she calls evangelical, orthodox Christians, are much too narrow in intellect to ever understand the Creator Principle. For her there is no heaven or hell, but rather one great place where all the souls of humankind will rest.

"Where did you get that, Mabel?"

"Why it's the logical deduction of examining the progress of the evolution of theological knowledge."

"That doesn't seem to line up with what the Bible says about God."

"Oh, my, that book has been so misinterpreted and mistranslated, it's hardly a reliable document for our age!"

Whoever Mabel's Prime Cause, and God-force is He (or maybe it's she) is not the same Lord God revealed in Scripture. And that means Mabel, for all her intellect, is caught up in idolatry.

And then there's Wayne. Basically, he is orthodox in his beliefs. He certainly has received Christ into his life. But his danger is a prevalent one in many lives today. "I just don't think God is that way!" he insists. But we are not allowed the freedom to conjure up imaginary characteristics for a very real God. He is true to the nature He reveals to us in His Word. Wayne's motives for not allowing God to be God must be dealt with or he risks committing idolatry and facing God's just anger.

Idolatry stems from our desire to control God. We want Him in our image so we can understand everything He thinks and does. We want Him personally tailored to our specifications, so we will not have to change. We want a God who favors our particular sin, so we will have no need of repentance. Our God is to be a flexible clay doll to keep on the shelf and remold when the mood suits us.

"Oh, I'm sure God isn't that way," we say, as we gouge and reshape our little clay figure.

If we can limit God to our design, we can have the best of all worlds. He can be great and mighty and powerful when we need His help. But we can keep Him out of our way when we sense His displeasure.

So, how can you and I make sure we have a proper view of God, avoid idolatry, and escape His just anger?

1. Review our sources for knowledge of God.

There is only one inerrant source: the Bible. We can be overly influenced by persuasive teaching, powerful writing, dramatic artwork. The compelling arguments of forceful teachers of psychology, science, anthropology, philosophy, etc., can all paint for us an unreal picture.

We can tell if our image of God is based on the Bible. Just give a chapter and verse to back up every attribute of God we can think of.

2. Be willing to accept whatever the Bible says about God.

When you and I read the Scriptures, we must continue to ask, what am I learning about God's nature, God's ways, God's very character? If the Bible says Jesus is God (John 1:1–5; 20:28) then that's the God we will worship. If the Bible says God will condemn all unrepentant sinners and cast them to everlasting hell (Matthew 25:46; Revelation

20:15) then it will be such a God we serve. If the Bible says God does not wish that any would have to face that fate (2 Peter 3:9), then it is to such a One as this that we will volunteer our services to reach the lost.

3. Meditate on the Bible record of who God is.

This will mean consistent, daily study of God's Word, and quiet times to reflect on what we have learned. It will mean memorizing verses, prayers of praise, and songs of glory. It will mean you and I concentrate as much on growing in true knowledge of God, as we do in growing in knowledge of our mate, or our children, or our prayer partner at church.

4. Ask God for His help in guiding us on this quest.

This means we will need to open up our thoughts and ideas about His nature to the examination of the Holy Spirit. Let Him point out the weaknesses in our view of His character. Commit ourselves to the lifetime adventure of learning more about God.

God's Anger in the New Testament

"But," some might protest, "all this talk about God's anger, it sounds so, so, Old Testament! Jesus came to take care of God's anger, didn't He? So we don't have to worry about all this anymore. After all, Jesus never got angry."

What?

Yes, Jesus came to satisfy God's just anger against sinners. In the Bible that's called *propitiation.*

However, to consider God's anger as only an Old Testament attribute, well, that means we now serve a different God, *or* a God who changes His personality.

Neither is true.

Jesus never gets angry? Wait a minute. How about that time men and animals ran for their lives to escape His fury?

Remember that scene?

It's found in all four gospels. John 2:15–16 states it this way: "He made a whip out of cords, and drove all from the temple area, both sheep and cattle; he scattered the coins of the money changers, and overturned their tables. To those who sold doves he said, 'Get these out of here! How dare you turn my Father's house into a market!' "

Was Jesus actually angry?

Yep.

Was it because of idolatry?

Nope. But it was something just as bad. God's holiness was being abused and He was not about to let it go unchecked.

According to Mark 11, Jesus entered the magnificent temple (built by Herod the Great) on the day of His triumphant last ride into Jerusalem. We call it Palm Sunday. He peered around intently, then left. The sight that He saw undoubtedly dominated His mind for the rest of the evening. Even amidst the warmth and hospitality of friends in Bethany, the temple scene would not go away. Perhaps those thoughts tossed and turned in His mind throughout the night and moved Him to leave the house the next morning before breakfast and head back into Jerusalem. By the time He hiked across the Kidron Valley and up to the city, it must have been obvious to those around Him that Jesus was angry.

The temple area dominated the Jerusalem landscape. The twenty-five acre complex was perched on the crown of Mt. Zion. The temple, rising to 150 feet, was the city's jewel. Here at the temple, God revealed Himself to His chosen people. Even a casual traveler through the city would be attracted to the structure, perhaps even drawn to marvel at the God who was worshiped there.

Jewish pilgrims flocked to Jerusalem by the thousands. Scattered across the Mediterranean region, they held on to their desire to worship at the temple through the centuries. Both Jews and God-fearing Gentiles streamed in from

The Surprising Side of Grace

Parthia, Media, Elam, Mesopotamia, Cappadocia, Pontus, Asia, Phrygia, Pamphylia, Egypt, Libya, Cyrene, Arabia, Crete, and Rome. They came to offer true worship to the true God. What a glorious time of celebration! And surely if any season was a good one to spend in worship in the temple, the Passover was the best of all. This memorial of God's miraculous deliverance of His people from bondage in Egypt summed up all the pilgrims' hopes that Israel once again would be free.

But such a pilgrimage was not cheap. The expense of travel, a place to stay, and food to eat quickly added up. The temple regulations further depleted their resources. The annual temple tax of one-half shekel was required of all Jewish men and proselytes. The official coin was the only one accepted. That meant exchanging the Greek and Roman silver for the sacred, or temple, shekel. A fee was charged for this service of converting money. Crooked dealing was common as worshipers tried counting their change in an unfamiliar monetary system. Arguments and shouts punctuated the temple atmosphere. In the very area where Gentiles should be attracted to view the house of the one true God—and pay respects to the Lord Almighty—coin exchange booths were installed. They must have looked as ludicrous as a row of slot machines in a Nevada supermarket.

In addition, animal inspectors crowded around to check each sacrifice according to temple standards. Flawed or imperfect animals they rejected. Each inspector charged a fee for his service. The pilgrims were forced to barter and haggle here, too. Fine distinctions often disqualified an animal. Heated debate enlivened the air. If you wished to avoid the hassle of the inspectors, you could purchase an animal that had already been inspected. Such animals were sold at an exorbitant price, of course.

Other items sold in the Court of the Gentiles included the wine, oil, salt, and incense needed for the sacrifices.

Many travelers used the temple area for a shortcut into the city. Merchants from Jericho and the Jordan River valley passed through on their way to the heart of Jerusalem. God's sacred site had turned into a busy thoroughfare and bazaar.

On the very site where people should have been drawn into a closer fellowship with God, the shouts and curses flowed.

Jesus was righteously, violently angry.

He gathered a bundle of reeds and whacked the animals.

He flung coins onto the stone floor.

He kicked over tables of merchandise.

He emptied the stalls.

People scattered everywhere. Others froze in fright. Some cowered against the wall, and many fled right out the gates of the temple area and into the city.

A wild man was on the loose and no one dared stop Him. No one called for the troops at the fortress, Antonia, that adjoined the Temple. No one attempted to arrest Him (even though Sadducees, Pharisees, and Herodians had been wanting to for months).

Is this the same Jesus who held babies in His arms?

Is this the Jesus who healed the sick?

Is this the Jesus who would offer no defense when He was brought to trial and threatened with crucifixion?

Is this the Jesus who said, "Do not resist an evil person. If someone strikes you on the right cheek, turn to him the other also" (Matthew 5:39), and "Love your enemies and pray for those who persecute you" (Matthew 5:44)?

Yep. It's the same Jesus. Instead of finding a sacred gathering of folks seeking the Father in prayer and worship, He finds a blasphemous marketplace. And Jesus is furious.

A holy ground, which had been set aside for God's special purposes, had been made common, ordinary, and profane. Jesus said, "You have made it a 'den of robbers' " (Mark 11:17). By doing this He compared those in charge of the temple with the vicious, savage bandits that ambushed weary travelers along the Judean wilderness route. The authorities had abdicated their responsibility and showed little regard for God's holiness.

Moses at the burning bush took off his shoes and was afraid to look at God (Exodus 3:5–6). Isaiah before God's throne felt worthless, ashamed of his sin (Isaiah 6:5). The outer courtyard of the Gentiles might not compare to the burning bush or God's literal throne room, but it was, nonetheless, sacred. Here was a place set apart, where man's attention should have focused on the glorious attributes of an almighty God. But most thought only of monetary gains to be made in buying and selling. They cared more about a good deal than a good God.

In addition, they showed disrespect for God's people. Why did the pilgrims travel for miles to this place? Not to spend time in the merchant stalls. Not to spend energy fighting for a fair price with the temple inspector. The only officials needed in that area should have been those who could assist worshipers in the knowledge and praise of the Almighty. The obvious hypocrisy must have hardened hearts that had originally been open to true worship. A casual observer must have concluded that perhaps this God cared more about money than souls.

A further aspect of the offense was the misuse of the physical grounds. The temple was holy because God had chosen to dwell there. He revealed Himself to His people at this very place. Certainly the world has boasted more magnificent buildings throughout history. But this specific plot of real estate was set aside for God's unique and special purpose. The whole temple area deserved utmost respect. But the smell of stalls and the stench of greed overpowered the aroma of incense and ascending prayers.

The temple's been gone from Jerusalem for over nineteen hundred years now. We might feel that we can safely escape His anger over such abused holiness. But maybe we need only look down the street, around the corner, or across town—wherever our particular church might be. It, too, is holy ground that has been set aside for the special purpose for which God intended it. Church leaders today have a righteous burden to maintain the holiness of their ministry. Selection by the people of God as they seek His will to a leadership role isn't the same as being elected to the board of directors of a corporation. A leader's ministry, whether called Bishop, Elder, Pastor, or Deacon, is to lead the congregation into a deepening relationship with God, our Father. It's an awesome and challenging responsibility.

How We Can Keep Our Churches From Abusing God's Holiness

1. We should focus our ministry, time, and money on the necessary functions of church life.

What are those? Dr. John F. MacArthur, Jr. offers some sound advice when he suggests the following pattern in his book *Ashamed of the Gospel* (Crossway Books, Wheaton, IL, 1993, chapter 9):

a. Godly leadership—talented teachers of God's Word who live open, holy lives.

b. Biblical goals—such as worship, spiritual growth, evangelism, fellowship.

c. Discipleship—learning how to solve everyday problems by applying Scripture to life.

d. Outreach—consistently challenging the lost around us to come to a saving knowledge of Christ.

e. Concern for one another—actively, biblically, involved in the lives of other believers.

f. Commitment to the family—helping individuals build strong, healthy family life.

51

g. Biblical teaching and preaching—upholding God's Word and commanding that it be obeyed.

h. A willingness to change—never letting traditions thwart the implementation of biblical truth.

i. Worship—the coming together of God's people to give Him honor and praise, to set before Him our concerns, and to listen attentively to His.

With an atmosphere of complete acceptance that reassures everyone that they have entered their spiritual home—with programs that allow and equip each person to use God-given gifts to their fullest ability—with worship that lifts participants into God's throne room, that catches them up in His presence where they can experience His love, correction, and forgiveness—it's difficult to imagine such a church having much problem abusing God's holiness.

2. We must make proper use of the physical facilities that we have set aside for God's holy purposes.

We offend God when we misuse physical items and places of worship. Some might protest that the place of worship does not matter much, it's the attitude of believer that counts. It is true that the primary requirement for worship that pleases God is to worship Him in spirit and truth (John 4:24). But once an earthly facility is dedicated to God, it becomes His possession. Have we given each church building and all of its rooms to Him? Have we offered our hymnbooks, communion table, baptistery, and pulpit for His use? From boiler-room to bell tower, it belongs to Him.

That being so, we must learn to use the facilities in a way that is compatible with His will and His nature. All activities using God's facilities and His furnishings should neither violate His character nor invite His displeasure.

3. We must be careful to insure that distractions are eliminated from worship.

In the busy atmosphere of the temple area, Jesus found it was almost impossible for anyone to concentrate on God.

Some modern churches aren't too much different.

A prayerful analysis of our church buildings and worship services might reveal useless clutter and disruptive elements that prevent our minds and hearts from being attentive to God's presence. *is not in the building*

Is the design of your church important? The Old Testament devotes whole chapters to the minute details of the tabernacle and temple designs. Although biblical blueprints don't exist for modern churches, we should use considerable care when deciding on their shape and form.

Insufficient repair and upkeep also insults God's holiness. How do we furnish God's house compared to our own homes? Is our church the repository for worn chairs, tattered rugs, scarred tables, and broken-down couches? Some donate these with sanctimonious fanfare. Meanwhile their dens shine with the latest color and style, and their tax form reports a nice write-off to God's house. *not a building*

God doesn't need an expensive house, but what we do for Him must be first-class. No one knows when the balcony railing will be repaired or the lights in the candelabra replaced or the cobwebs in the stained-glass window dusted. Anything less than excellent maintenance is a disgrace.

Tense bartering and the technical requirement of correct coins dulled free worship in Jesus' day. Complex worship forms or total lack of organization can also divert our full attention from the Lord. All members of the congregation must feel that they have been confronted by the Almighty.

The temple abusers forgot that the Lord God lived among them. Those things dedicated to God must be kept holy. We should enter His house with praise and thanksgiving. We should come before His presence with trembling and awe. Anything less insults His dignity. Anything less isn't worship in spirit and truth to an all-knowing, all-powerful, ever-present, personal, loving, forgiving heavenly Father. Anything less abuses God's holiness, which, like idolatry, is a very quick path to experiencing God's anger.

Some things should be just that obvious.

Living the Word

1. Why do you think idolatry is still a problem in all societies today? *People allow many forms of idoltry exhalt itself above the knowledge of God.*

2. Read the following verses. What do they say about idolatry? 1 Corinthians 5:11; 6:9; Colossians 3:5. *Do not associate с idoltere. They will not inherit the kingdom of God. Put away idoltry*

3. Study Romans 1:18–32. According to this passage, from where does idolatry come? And where does God allow it to lead? *Suppressed truth, which leads to wickedness. God gave them over to a depraved mind.*

4. Review Haggai 1:1–11. What guidelines can be found here for the way we should build and maintain our churches?

Not relevant Lack of understanding on the authors part!

5. On a scale of one to ten, how important is actual experience of worship in your life? On the same scale, how important did worship of the Father seem to be to Jesus while He was here on earth? Still using that scale, how important do you think worship will be in heaven? What do those answers tell you?

6. Consider making Psalm 103:1–5 your prayer:

> *Praise the LORD, O my soul; all my inmost being, praise his holy name. Praise the LORD, O my soul, and forget not all his benefits—who forgives all your sins and heals all your diseases, who redeems your life from the pit and crowns you with love and compassion, who satisfies your desires with good things so that your youth is renewed like the eagle's.*

Kindness leads us toward repentance Roman 2:4

Chapter 4

Whatever Happened to Justice and Mercy?

What do you do when you get angry?

Is your behavior predictable?

Ask those around you. Some rant and rave, some sulk away in silence, some bang their fist on the table (or anything else that is handy), some curse and wave their hands, some stalk through the house, slamming doors. What do you do?

When it's my behavior that has caused the problem, I have a tendency to call myself names. "Insensitive jerk!" seems to come out fairly easy.

I suppose we all have a tendency to call ourselves names—or, more often, call other people names—when we're expressing our anger. Now name-calling doesn't seem like the Christian thing to do. And it's usually followed by a wave of guilt over the fact that we lost control of the situation.

What did Jesus do when He got angry?

Sometimes, He called people names.

"He did what?"

You'll find the account in Matthew 23:23–24: "Woe to you, teachers of the law and Pharisees, you hypocrites! You give a tenth of your spices—mint, dill and cumin. But you have neglected the more important matters of the law—

justice, mercy and faithfulness. You should have practiced the latter, without neglecting the former. You blind guides! You strain out a gnat but swallow a camel."

Hypocrites and blind guides? That strong language severely offended those who were so accused.

But it was meant to do just that. Jesus was angry.

A scribe (teacher of the Mosaic Law) was one who had the task of copying and supervising the copying of the sacred Old Testament Scriptures. This important position required attention to every detail of each individual letter. Since the scribes knew the Scriptures so well, they were often consulted concerning the meaning of the Law. They became the official experts on religious law—the lawyers of their day. They taught, answered questions, and served on the supreme court, the Sanhedrin.

Their teaching usually consisted of a rehash of what had been written before them. They held high academic and social positions. They paid close attention to their own concerns and advancements. Jesus circumvented their hard-earned position and paid little attention to their stilted discussions. They, in turn, hated Him.

The Pharisees were a religious/political party in Judea. They were the "set-apart ones." They were not fatalistic like the Essenes who lived at Qumran, or free-thinking and worldly like the Sadducees. The Pharisees believed in such things as the resurrection, angels and demons, and future rewards and punishments. Jesus had little disagreement with them on those points.

But He did actively oppose the Pharisees whenever their traditions invalidated God's Word: "You nullify the word of God by your tradition that you have handed down. And you do many things like that" (Mark 7:13). He graphically pointed out when they failed to show compassion to all people, " 'Which of these three do you think was a neighbor to the man who fell into the hands of robbers?' The expert in the law replied, 'The one who had mercy on him.' Jesus told him, 'Go and do likewise' " (Luke 10:36–37). He would not leave unchallenged their practice of preferring ritual, tradition, and prejudice over empathy and benevolence. "If any of you has a sheep and it falls into a pit on the Sabbath, will you not take hold of it and lift it out? How much more valuable is a man than a sheep!" (Matthew 12:11–12).

The Pharisees used their traditions (and tried to use Scriptures) to back up their defense against Jesus. He knew better. They were not motivated by a desire for true holiness, but by jealousy over Jesus' success. They loved the approval of men more than the approval of God. He told them that they misunderstood the true meaning of Scripture and therefore the power of God.

So He called them a name.

Hypocrite.

What He meant was that they were polluted, impious, unfaithful, unprincipled in the things of God while professing godliness and piety. They were actually antagonistic to all that was sacred, true, and godly.

They, of course, understood exactly what He meant by the term. They plotted to have Him killed.

But what was the particular offense that made Jesus so angry in the original scene? They proved how spiritual they were by a public demonstration of their tithing. Not only did they give ten percent of their income to the Lord, but they gave ten percent of everything—even to the extreme of weighing out the spices and dividing the flakes of herbs that they grew in the garden. They pointed out such practices to prove their piety.

Jesus never once claimed that tithing was wrong. And He didn't condemn the practice of giving a portion of even a small and insignificant item. The teachers of the law and the Pharisees were faithful money givers. They knew how to dole it out to their best advantage. They sounded trumpets. They proclaimed their generosity in loud public prayer.

The Surprising Side of Grace

The problem was, they ignored other commands that are much more central to faith and practice than tithing spices.

Jesus was angry because they neglected justice, mercy, and faithfulness.

Justice: Seeing that individuals received fair treatment; insisting that punishment or reward fit the deed, with the standard of measurement being the Word of God.

"Evil men do not understand justice, but those who seek the LORD understand it fully" (Proverbs 28:5).

Mercy: Showing goodness and love for the guilty and miserable, giving back a measure of what we have received from God.

"I desire mercy, not sacrifice" (Hosea 6:6).

Faithfulness: Being absolutely reliable; not two-faced or fickle; completely loyal in obedience to God.

"Let love and faithfulness never leave you; bind them around your neck, write them on the tablet of your heart" (Proverbs 3:3).

It is almost inconceivable that anyone would consider tithing two sprinkles of paprika and oregano to be a more important spiritual duty than practicing justice, mercy, and faithfulness. That it's the teachers of the law and the Pharisees—the self-appointed religious leaders of the people—who are guilty is inexcusable. They busied themselves with the trivia of the faith and ignored those matters that are closest to the heart of God.

We might, from a distance, excuse them as misguided or ignorant of God's priorities.

But Jesus didn't give them that benefit.

He was mad.

Real mad.

Seven times in Matthew 23 he "woes" them. And when you get "woed" by Jesus, your future is sealed. In Matthew 11:21 he woes the towns of Korazin and Bethsaida, and today they are wiped off the face of the earth.

How angry is Jesus? Judge for yourself. Near the conclusion of His Matthew 23 tirade, Jesus says, "You snakes! You brood of vipers! How will you escape being condemned to hell?" (Matthew 23:33). Can you imagine looking into the eyes of the only begotten Son of God and have Him say that to you? Can you think of any words He could have used to make His feelings more clear?

But you and I have a hard time learning to tithe our money, let alone the mint that grows out back, so we feel immune from the condemnation of Matthew 23. But the real problem does persist today in the lives of religious people. We can still spend so much time on the peripheries of the faith that we neglect the central core.

We can still spend our lives legalistically scrutinizing others' lives and completely neglect justice, mercy, and faithfulness.

Symptoms of a Life
Without Justice and Mercy

1. Insensitivity to others, especially those who are different from us.

My time was divided between staring at the tiny baby ahead of me and gazing at a row of neatly displayed toothbrushes. I waited with little patience at the drugstore counter. All I wanted were some breath mints, and then I needed to hurry back to the church office. The baby must have been about three months old. He kept crying and only stopped for an occasional deep cough. The mother tried to comfort him the best she could.

At her side were two other youngsters, neither one of them school age. They held on to their mother's worn skirt and peered at the rows of toys on the far wall. At long last the clerk returned from a storeroom and looked at us. "Good afternoon, Reverend Bly," she said, looking past the lady with the baby. "My, you're dressed up today."

59

The Surprising Side of Grace

I was wearing my dark western suit, a black leather vest, and my dressiest cowboy boots. Pinned to my lapel was a white boutonniere. "Yes, I have a wedding at 2:00," I reported, glancing at my watch. "But this lady is first." I pointed to the anxious mother.

"Oh? Well, what do you want?" the clerk snapped at the lady. Several sentences in Spanish accompanied the waving of a prescription. The clerk reached for the paper, but the lady wouldn't let go.

"Look, Reverend, I'd better take care of you. She'll be here for an hour and you'll be late for your wedding." Punching the cash register, she looked at me. "That'll be ninety-three cents."

"Well, eh, sure," I stammered and handed her the change.

As I picked up the breath mints and headed for the door, I could hear the mother get very agitated. She desperately tried to communicate. My high-school Spanish started to kick in as I exited. *"Quantos dinero por esta receta? Tango solamente cinco dolares."*

Having only five dollars, the woman was afraid she didn't have enough to pay for the medicine.

I should have returned and explained the situation to the clerk. Then, if the prescription was more than five bucks, I should have offered to pay the rest.

Yeah, I should have.

It's called justice and mercy.

But I hurried down the street to the church so I could wait for a young lady, who had paid $2,000 for a dress she would wear once in her life.

That was sixteen years ago, and the pleading face of a young mother asking *"Quantos dinero?"* still haunts me. I failed at a simple little test of mercy and justice.

2. Ignorance of the needs of others.

Cindy spent her student-teaching months in the inner-city. That was a shocking experience for a farm girl raised near a town of 3,000 people. She brought home stories of poverty, filth, violence, prejudice, and despair. Her parents worried for her safety. Then, they began to grow indignant about the conditions. "We've got to get folks at church organized to help those poor families in the city!" they decided.

One day a new schoolteacher at the local, small-town school stopped by to visit Cindy's parents. They told him of the conditions where their daughter worked.

"Hey, that's right where I grew up!" he exclaimed.

"I bet you're glad to get out of all that poverty!" her dad posed.

"Actually," the man said cautiously, "I've never seen poverty as bad as we have it here in this town. Yesterday I took a little girl home from school, sick. She lives in one of those little shacks behind the stores on Central Street. A family of six lives in two cold cement rooms. There's no heat, one bare light bulb, no cupboards, no chairs, no drapes, no beds, and cardboard covering up a broken window. They offered me a cup of coffee—I think it was the only thing they had in the house to give. No wonder the little girl was sick. I never saw anything like that where I grew up."

Showing justice and mercy are much easier at a distance.

Do you know who in your own town, city, or neighborhood needs desperately to experience some justice and mercy? Sometimes we don't even know the needs around us.

Jesus knows.

3. Busyness with personal concerns.

Mercy and justice take time.

And we are convinced that "time is money." We aren't about to give away time or money, let alone allow someone to steal it from us.

I was still fifty miles from home when I saw them along the side of the highway. A bewildered family stood around

61

an old car whose hood was up, waiting for the revival of a dead motor. I had been away from home for over a week, on a speaking trip. Exhausted from an eight-hour drive, all I wanted to do was get home and be with my family.

Surely a state patrolman would stop and help them.

I flew past them for a mile or two, then felt the Lord prick my conscience.

I turned around.

When I arrived, the father held a broken fan belt in his hand. I asked him if I could help.

He just stared.

His ten-year-old daughter replied that he did not speak English, so she became the interpreter. Soon, the whole family crowded into the cab of my pickup and we headed for the nearest town.

It was two towns, four service stations, and two parts-stores later when we found a belt that would fit. We filled a couple of cans with water and headed back out to the highway. It was nearly two hours from the time I had stopped before I was ready to get back on the road and head for home.

A lively discussion ensued between the husband and wife. Then the daughter explained, "My father wants you to have this money."

I gently refused.

Mercy has its own reward.

I like to believe there was a smile and a nod around the throne room of heaven that day. I had finally gotten it right. I was doing the important things.

4. Inordinate desire to maintain the status quo.

Maybe this was what the Pharisee and others hated most about Jesus. He kept rocking the boat.

And, thousands of years later, He's still tying to get us to shake up our schedules and pay a little more attention to justice and mercy.

But most of us like things just the way they are.

Larry volunteered to serve on a church committee that was given the responsibility of sponsoring a refugee family. He was perfect for the position. As a successful realtor, he knew every housing situation in town. Larry attended only one meeting after church on Sunday. The task force then decided to meet on Monday nights, which, as every neglected wife knows, is football night. He was not about to change his Monday night ritual, no matter how many hurting, frightened refugees needed his assistance.

Lorraine works at a dress shop. She takes her lunch hour from 11:30 to 12:30. That's been her practice for almost twenty years. She beats the noon rush at The Pantry that way. When her co-worker, Carol, asked to switch lunch breaks, Lorraine got in a huff. "How dare she ask me to change! I certainly have seniority around here!" Carol explained that her three-year-old was enrolled in a pre-school that ended at 11:30. The switch would allow Carol to pick up little Katherine and take her to her grandmother's.

Lorraine, who sits on the center aisle in the third pew and sings in the living Christmas tree at First Church, refused. She didn't bother asking the Lord's opinion. Maybe she knew what He would say. A God whose very essence is mercy doesn't approve of children who show none of it themselves.

5. Selective legalism.

In all the advancements of civilization and philosophical thought, no one has come up with a more concise definition of justice than the Old Testament phrase, "Life for life, eye for eye, tooth for tooth, hand for hand, foot for foot" (Deuteronomy 19:21).

The verse is not a license for dismemberment, but a graphic illustration that the punishment ought to fit the crime. No more, no less. That's what we still call justice.

And that justice was always meant to be universally applied. "You are to have the same law for the alien and the native-born. I am the LORD your God" (Leviticus 24:22).

The Surprising Side of Grace

Now we all subscribe to that form of justice, right?

Ted is a well-known lawyer. Recently, as district attorney, he prosecuted a young man involved in a theater riot.

A violent gang movie had been shown in a tense urban area. Emotions ran high. A fight broke out in the lobby. Someone got stabbed. Three days later the victim died. A frightened seventeen-year-old named Devon turned himself in. He described his mounting fear while watching the movie, and the taunts of antagonizers around him who threatened him and the girl he was with. He claimed to have pulled the knife in self-defense.

After all the evidence was in, Ted pushed to get Devon tried as an adult. Then he pressed for and got a conviction of second-degree murder. The public defender pleaded that prison would destroy the boy, but Ted emphasized the fact that Devon brought an illegal weapon into the theater and stressed his prior misdemeanor convictions. "He should be an example to the others of what will happen if they persist with such violence!" Several weeks later Devon attempted suicide while in jail.

Last spring the community was shocked to discover that Ted was himself arrested for suspicion of attempted murder. It seems that several teens had been loitering around the alley behind his home, and he suspected that they might be trying to break into his garage. He got jittery and tried to scare them off by waving a gun at them.

Ted reported that the gun accidentally discharged and struck the back of one of the boys in the alley. He was first accused of felonious assault, but the charges were soon greatly reduced. The sentence was probation. Jail was out of the question. After all, wasn't it self-defense? Besides, Ted is such an important leader in the community.

Devon, and the young man with a bullet in his back, might complain that there is no justice in all of this.

I think they're right. It would be hard to explain such actions to God.

6. A low view of the redemptive power of God.

Most of the time we like justice and we distrust mercy.

Most times. Except when applied to us, of course.

"Don't give 'em a break," we demand. "Make 'em pay for their mistake! They deserve it!"

"Don't fall for that change-of-heart garbage! They're just using you to weasel out of what they deserve!"

But God does change people.

He changes them radically.

Sharon moved in with Gary to find excitement. What she found was a heroin habit instead. Eighteen months later she moved back in with her parents, along with her six-month-old daughter. Her good job at the finance company ended when they suspected her of embezzling. She stole from her mother, cashed forged checks, passed off family charge cards, and rifled bank accounts. She had a six-times-a-day habit to support.

Finally, her mother had her arrested. She could not stand to see Sharon drag little Katie around in that kind of world. Her mother hoped and prayed that Sharon would get some help. While incarcerated, Sharon called out to God for the first time in her life. She began to notice a change inside herself immediately. The courts were not impressed with her "jailhouse conversion."

Probation was continually denied, no matter how much of a model prisoner Sharon became. Finally, for some inexplicable reason, a skeptical judge reversed her opinion and allowed Sharon to finish her sentence at a Christian drug rehabilitation center. She finished the program, free from drugs, free to start her life over again. The scars of needles still marked her arms, but the redemptive power of God was working in her heart.

She came back home and began attending church with her mother. But when she volunteered to help with the youth group, she was told that many parents felt she would be a bad influence on their teens.

They had forgotten God's power and judged her to be outside the scope of His help.

7. Radically narrow focus of the ministry of the church.

In the previous chapter I mentioned a few of the main priorities of church life. Now it's time to add another. In the midst of all of the other functions, we must be a lighthouse of justice, mercy, and faithfulness.

Two hundred fifty ranch workers were fired in one day and given two weeks' notice to vacate company housing. Many protested. They stayed in their homes. A court battle raged. Meanwhile, the gas and electricity in the houses were turned off. Families cooked on charcoal stoves and awaited the judge's decision.

Through the school principal I learned that many of the children were coming to school with inadequate winter clothing. I made an appeal during a church service for clothing and blankets. Harry did not like that one bit. The next day in my office he graphically explained the complexity of the situation and said the owners were not to blame for the firings or the shutoff of the utilities. "We can't take sides in this!" he roared.

I told him I appreciated the information, but believed we still needed to do something about the freezing children. Their learning and health were at stake. Therefore, I reasoned, it was our duty to help.

"But most of them don't speak English! They aren't even Christians!" he shouted.

Harry was right about that, but he overlooked the fact that the Bible does not limit justice and mercy only to those who believe. Harry would not hesitate to bring the same children on the church bus to attend vacation Bible school. But to provide clothing for them at such a time as this, in Harry's mind, allied us with the workers in what he considered a political protest.

Lots of us can get into a similar trap. Overemphasize religious busywork, forget about mercy. Don't be concerned with socially complex things like justice. What does all this have to do with faithfulness, anyway?

Folks living 700 years before Christ's visit to earth had the same problem. Micah made it clear to them what was important to God, "He has showed you, O man, what is good. And what does the LORD require of you? To act justly and to love mercy and to walk humbly with your God" (6:8).

It is the neglect of this command that draws Jesus' just anger in Matthew 23.

For some of us, there needs to be a refocus of our concern with justice and mercy, without losing sight of the other important ministries that the Lord has set before us.

Getting Back on Track With Justice and Mercy

• In the past thirty days, which of your activities would be interpreted by those around you as a clear stand for biblical justice and mercy?

• During the last six months, can you remember a time when you said, "That's not fair! Somebody ought to do something!" while you, in fact, did nothing?

• If you noticed any failure on your part from these reflections, stop and confess that failure before the Lord.

• Ask a good Christian friend to take an objective look at your priorities and activities. If he or she finds you spending a disproportionate amount of time with minor religious activities, have him or her point that out to you. If such things exist, ask God to help you dedicate yourself to matters that are more important to Him.

• For the next month, add this to your daily prayer: "Lord, when You look at my neighborhood, my community, my church, what touches Your heart most about the needs of these people? Touch my heart in the same way."

67

The Surprising Side of Grace

There are times when we are motivated to obey God's injunctions in order to avoid His displeasure. There's nothing evil or unbiblical about such an incentive. If you have no other reason for actively pursuing justice and mercy than to escape His wrath, that's an honest justification for your behavior.

Yet, just as injustice will anger the soul of a spiritual man, so there is a deep joy in seeing justice triumph. It is a signal-bell to the world that there are rules and absolutes which cannot be violated without consequence.

And the Holy Spirit within us confirms a deep satisfaction when biblical mercy is shown. The angels in heaven rejoice at the mercy of God shown to one sinner who repents. So every act of biblical mercy should elicit a shout of victory from each of us.

We must work for the day that mercy and justice flow from our words and deeds for the sheer pleasure of delighting God.

He deserves that kind of child.

Living the Word

1. Review the Seven Symptoms of a Life Without Justice and Mercy listed in this chapter. With which one(s) of these do you struggle at the present time? Why?

Busyness & personal concerns
Hurley - sickness.

2. Study 2 Corinthians 7:11. What does this say about where motivation for justice should begin?

With us.

3. Do you pass by the bell-ringer for a local charity at Christmas without giving anything? Why? If not, why do you stop and donate?

I do give to Salvation army, but sometimes I do pass by.

I want to help those less

fortunate & I realize & blessing comes
responsibility?

4. Read Isaiah 1:15–17. In what way could this passage apply to your country? Your community? Your own church? Your life? If it does apply in any of these areas, what can you personally do about the situation?

The Stand our country has taken on abortion.

5. Why do you think Jesus combines justice, mercy, and faithfulness in the Matthew 23:23 passage? Is there a conflict among these qualities? If not, how do they complement each other?

6. You might like to make Psalm 5:1–8 your prayer:

> *Give ear to my words, O LORD, consider my sighing. Listen to my cry for help, my King and my God, for to you I pray. Morning by morning, O LORD, you hear my voice; morning by morning I lay requests before you and wait in expectation. You are not a God who takes pleasure in evil; with you the wicked cannot dwell. The arrogant cannot stand in your presence; you hate all who do wrong. You destroy those who tell lies; bloodthirsty and deceitful men the LORD abhors. But I, by your great mercy, will come into your house; in reverence will I bow down toward your holy temple. Lead me, O LORD, in your righteousness because of my enemies—make straight your way before me.*

Chapter 5

Life in a Blurred Society

The now-famous home video showed several police-men beating up an African-American. Was it police brutal-ity, or justifiable restraint?

A television news camera caught on tape several Afri-can-Americans bashing a white truck driver's head with a brick. Is it attempted murder, or a justifiable reaction to a riotous condition?

What's right?

What's wrong?

Sometimes it seems like we live in a blurred society.

Where does our society stand on moral issues?

Abortions are legal; killing a spotted owl is illegal.

Distributing condoms on campus to teenagers is legal; passing out Bibles at public schools is illegal.

Inviting homosexuals into the classroom to explain their lifestyle is encouraged; teaching abstinence as the safest and best method of preventing sexually transmitted diseases is not encouraged.

The top ten movies in video sales last week included four G-rated cartoon features, three PG-rated children's movies, and three tapes of nude women in provocative poses.

We live in a morally blurred society.

Fortunately, there is a place to turn where moral issues are dealt with in a clear manner. A place where right is always right, and wrong is always wrong.

God's Word speaks clearly to the issues of our day.
Perhaps too clearly.

1 • "You shall have no other gods before me" (Exodus 20:3).

2 • "You shall not make for yourself an idol in the form of anything in heaven above or on the earth beneath or in the waters below" (Exodus 20:4).

3 • "You shall not misuse the name of the LORD your God, for the LORD will not hold anyone guiltless who misuses his name" (Exodus 20:7).

4 • "Remember the Sabbath day by keeping it holy" (Exodus 20:8).

5 • "Honor your father and your mother, so that you may live long in the land the LORD your God is giving you" (Exodus 20:12).

6 • "You shall not murder" (Exodus 20:13).

7 • "You shall not commit adultery" (Exodus 20:14).

8 • "You shall not steal" (Exodus 20:15).

9 • "You shall not give false testimony against your neighbor" (Exodus 20:16).

10 • "You shall not covet" (Exodus 20:17).

The tough part of the Ten Commandments is not in trying to understand what they mean. Right and wrong is obvious here. The difficult part is trying to live out what we know God demands.

The problem with biblical wisdom has never been that it's difficult to understand (as some would suggest). The real dilemma is that it's, most often, frightfully easy to understand. Notice how the New Testament avoids ambivalence as well.

"The acts of the sinful nature are obvious: sexual immorality, impurity and debauchery; idolatry and witchcraft; hatred, discord, jealousy, fits of rage, selfish ambition, dissensions, factions and envy; drunkenness, orgies, and the like. I warn you, as I did before, that those who live like this will not inherit the kingdom of God" (Galatians 5:19–21).

71

Notice that Paul said it was obvious such actions were wrong. Elsewhere he is equally explicit:

"Do you not know that the wicked will not inherit the kingdom of God? Do not be deceived: Neither the sexually immoral nor idolaters nor adulterers nor male prostitutes nor homosexual offenders nor thieves nor the greedy nor drunkards nor slanderers nor swindlers will inherit the kingdom of God" (1 Corinthians 6:9–10).

Now some folks read such plain and transparent statements and claim that they are much too simplistic for our modern, complex society. What we often hear is the complaint that we are "offering simplistic answers to complicated questions." Thus with a wave of self-deluded superior intelligence some have dismissed any obligation to biblical morality. Such an act, of course, misses the issue.

Many answers are simple. That is, they are easy to figure out and evident to all.

The mistake is to assume that the issues involved are complex. The Bible offers simple answers to basic human problems. What better system could we have?

A simple problem is one that has a single cause.

Simple does not mean it's a minor matter. Nor does it mean it will be easy to correct. But it does mean the problem is solvable.

No matter how perplexing our dilemma might be, we have to listen to and abide by God's standards of human behavior.

How We Reject Biblical Morality

1. The argument from piety.

Hershel pastored a fast-growing church in southern California. He was a popular preacher. He had that rare ability to combine informal humor and straight Bible teaching. His calendar soon filled with speaking engagements from coast to coast. There were pastors' conferences in third-world countries, and homiletic lectures at seminaries. His national radio program spread the ministry, and a dozen books perched him on the verge of becoming a national Christian leader.

But there was an uneasy feeling among those who were close to the situation. Staff members of his church began to quit. After a while, he could never be reached directly, only through his secretary. Longtime friendships with other Christian leaders were dropped or ignored. Then it was rumored that his wife of twenty-four years had packed up the kids and moved to Florida.

Finally, a deacon in the church confronted Hershel. Then the story broke: he had been having an affair with his secretary for eight years. The church was devastated. His wife and children were crushed. Christians all around the country were forced to carry the pain of his failure.

Hershel did not hesitate to confess, but insisted that he was doing nothing wrong. "I prayed about this a long time. I've never felt God's leading more strongly. God wants us together, and I can't thwart God's will. We commit our relationship to Him in prayer whenever we get together."

The church was ripped apart.

Hershel is now remarried.

And still preaching.

Somehow, many believe that if they explain their own sin with pious words it will override God's Word. It's incredible how many try to demonstrate that their sin is God's will.

You can imagine what He thinks about this.

2. The argument from the perversion of Scripture.

Eddie became a Christian at the age of forty-five. Since then, the Lord has really blessed his construction business. At least, that's what Eddie claims. One thing's for sure—in the past ten years Eddie has certainly made a lot of money.

The Surprising Side of Grace

The twenty-four-room, two-story brick home on his ranch just outside of town supports this claim. The lighted tennis court alone cost $50,000. Whenever the church has a barbecue or picnic at Eddie's he's quick to say, "Isn't the Lord good for giving me all of this?"

Eddie's foreman of twelve years quit last month. He said that Eddie is too tight with his money. He would make excuses for not keeping workers too long, so he could avoid paying any more than the minimum wage. Short-term workers meant avoiding vacation time and health insurance.

Every time he confronted his boss about these things Eddie would go into a tirade about the foreman's ingratitude. Finally, he decided to quit when Eddie refused to upgrade the rental houses he owned (one of which the foreman rented). "The good Lord might have given him all that money, but He didn't give him the brains for how to use it," he concluded.

As far as Eddie was concerned, as long as he gave God credit for his wealth, then he could do with it whatever he pleased. "Jesus said that He came 'that they may have life, and have it to the full' [John 10:10], and that's what I'm doing," Eddie reported. "Living it to the full!"

"Greedy," "stingy," "uncompassionate" are words that come to mind, but Eddie doesn't see it that way. And he has, so he thinks, the Scriptures to back it up.

3. The argument from blindness.

Barbara owns a busy cafe on Main Street. That makes her a successful businessperson. But she's also an alcoholic. She doesn't admit that. She would, in fact, deny it on a stack of Bibles. Actually, she does just that every Sunday as she faithfully attends church with her children.

The folks down at the L&M Liquor Store know Barbara better than those at church. Every morning she stops by for a small bottle of vodka, and another of Tennessee whiskey.

Every morning.

Without fail.

The habit, she explains, came from growing up in the bitter winters of North Dakota. But one more Driving While Intoxicated offense and she'll be walking to work. She assures all around her that she has it under control.

Barbara often has folks at the café dump their personal problems on her, and she gives them her advice. "Their lives are all messed up and they don't pay attention to anything I say," she moans.

If she could see herself the way others see her—even better, if she could see herself the way the Lord sees her— she'd know why no one listens.

4. The argument from progressive wisdom.

The title of the lecture was "Morality for the Twenty-First Century." The speaker came from a prominent East Coast school of theology. His opening lines went something like this:

"The Bible was given to man by God as a general guideline for living. Primitive man had little notion of physical hygiene, civil behavior, or the dynamics of family psychology. They were instructed in language they could understand.

"That was then. And the Bible was fine . . . then.

"This is now. Today God speaks to us through science and technology. We must not refuse to listen to His voice," so the lecturer continued. "To be imprisoned in the morality of the Bible at the beginning of the twenty-first century is a tragedy of destructive proportions. It is a direct denial of God's progressive revelation to mankind!"

He had more to say about the need to change outdated institutions such as the traditional family, the church as we know it, and the government.

I don't know which bothered me more, that man's speech, or the applause of the audience throughout the speech.

Every clap, I assume, came from a person looking for an excuse to avoid the clear moral teaching of Scripture.

5. The argument from creation.

I never ask Robert about his wife anymore. I just don't know what to say. After twelve years of marriage, four children, and constant activity in church life, his wife Margie left him and the kids to move in with a twenty-two-year-old lesbian college girl with whom she was "madly in love."

She dropped out of the church but assured me her faith and love of the Lord was still strong. "God is the author of love, therefore, this must be according to His plan. After all, He created me this way. What else can I do? To reject this would be to insult the way He created me. They proved it's genetic, or something. I really can't do anything about it, you know?"

I guess she really believes that logic.

Paul wouldn't.

Neither do I.

6. The argument from ignorance.

Jack's on the road about three weeks out of every month. That's been his pattern for seventeen years. It's a long spell away from his wife and family, but he makes up for it, so he claims, during that intensive week when he's at home.

Over so many years he's developed quite a few habits that help him adjust to life on the road. But you won't get Jack to talk about all of them. He'll never tell you that he knows every adult book store in most every town through which he travels. He won't tell you about how many dollars he pumps into watching pornographic movies, nor how many magazines he's hidden in his suitcase next to his Bible and the letters from his wife.

"I don't think the Bible says anything about pornography, does it? I mean, it doesn't hurt anyone."

Jack honestly doesn't know what the Bible says about such literature. And he's not about to find out.

7. The argument from exemption.

Nancy's forty; her twins, Debbie and Dawn, are seventeen, Sally's fourteen, and Marc's twelve. She came into my office with what she called a "slight" dilemma.

"Well, before you laugh and tell me I should have known better you need to know I'm pregnant," she explained. "Look at me! Middle-age and expecting. Of course it's only a few weeks along. The kids don't know anything about it. But Bart and I have talked it through and we just don't think this is the right timing. My health hasn't been all that good, and the twins will be going to college soon. We're going to need both of us working. Now, as you know, I'm really opposed to abortions. But this, well, it's sort of like an exception. I've got to think about the other children—and Bart—and my own sanity. I think God understands, don't you, Pastor?"

Just how do you suppose God feels when we reject His standards of morality?

He doesn't leave us guessing about that either.

"Woe to those who call evil good and good evil, who put darkness for light and light for darkness, who put bitter for sweet and sweet for bitter. Woe to those who are wise in their own eyes and clever in their own sight" (Isaiah 5:20–21).

Now go back to the beginning of this chapter and review 1 Corinthians 6:9–10. This was just one list of behavior that God totally rejects. It included the sexually immoral, idolaters, adulterers, male prostitutes, homosexual offenders, thieves, greedy, drunkards, slanderers, and swindlers.

How many of these are still being called sinful, totally unacceptable behavior? And how many, even in some churches, are now considered permissible?

Do we really toss out teaching that seems so clear and direct?

One Christian denomination just drafted a proposal that supports an "open affirmation of gay and lesbian persons and their mutually loving, just, committed relationship of fidelity" (*Christianity Today*, November 22, 1993, page 43). In the same issue of the magazine (p. 38) it listed the open, heated debates taking place on five leading evangelical Christian college campuses over the issue of acceptance of homosexuality. In every case there were some who, while insisting on their commitment to Christ, claim that they see no contradiction between a biblical faith and their homosexual lifestyle.

That's exactly what Isaiah 5 meant when it lamented a people who call evil good and good evil. And homosexuality isn't the only behavior mentioned in that 1 Corinthians 6 list.

But just how angry does God get over such behavior?

Here's what Isaiah 5:24–25 reports:

"Therefore, as tongues of fire lick up straw and as dry grass sinks down in the flames, so their roots will decay and their flowers blow away like dust; for they have rejected the law of the LORD Almighty and spurned the word of the Holy One of Israel. Therefore the LORD's anger burns against his people; his hand is raised and he strikes them down. The mountains shake, and the dead bodies are like refuse in the streets. Yet for all this, his anger is not turned away, his hand is still upraised."

No matter what one's level of theological expertise might be, we all can understand this passage. God is angry.

How did He get so stirred up? A review of the first five chapters of Isaiah provides some clues. His anger stemmed from:

- rebellion against God (1:2, 5; 3:8).
- a lack of knowledge of their Lord (1:3; 5:13).
- despising God by turning away from Him (1:4; 2:8).
- speaking against the Lord (3:8).
- plundering the poor (3:14).
- women acting like prostitutes (3:16).
- undisciplined affluence (2:7; 5:8).
- drunkenness (5:11, 22).

- ignoring God's Word and work (5:12, 24).
- ridicule of God (5:19).
- being wise in their own eyes (5:21).
- rejecting God's laws (5:24).

All the time such things were happening, the people claimed to be doing nothing wrong. Not only that, they tried to persuade others to accept their standards, and they put down those who tried to do right. These were not heathens and barbarians. These were the chosen people of God. They were religious people who met for worship, and then lived out their weeks as though all was well between them and God.

He began to despise their burnt offerings and sacrifices. They were worthless to Him. And He was disgusted with their hypocritical worship. "Your New Moon festivals and your appointed feasts my soul hates. They have become a burden to me; I am weary of bearing them" (Isaiah 1:14).

God makes it clear.

There is right. There is wrong.

We come to church with phony worship if we insist on continuing to do wrong.

How to Reconstruct Your Moral Life

1. Seek the proper motivation for change.

Living a biblical moral life will not ensure our entrance into heaven. Eternal life is a gift from God when "you confess with your mouth, 'Jesus is Lord,' and believe in your heart that God raised him from the dead" (Romans 10:9).

But living a biblically moral life will bring big dividends. First, we will please our heavenly Father. Just as a child is eager to have a father watch his or her performance, so should we be motivated to please Him. We should long for a day when it can be said of us, as it was of the saints of old, "Therefore God is not ashamed to be called their God" (Hebrews 11:16).

Second, we should be motivated to live biblically moral lives because this is God's instruction book on building good relationships. Unbiblical morality destroys family life. It tears apart marriages and families. It undermines communities.

Biblical morality has a lasting positive effect. God shows love "to thousands who love me and keep my commandments" (Deuteronomy 5:10). Now that's an incredible promise. Talk about a life with lasting results. We must live biblically moral lives for our families today, and the generations to follow!

Third, we must live biblically moral lives for the sake of our own self-esteem and sanity. Rebellion against God's morality does catch up with us. The day comes to us, as it did to Paul, where we look at ourselves and say, "What a wretched man I am! Who will rescue me from this body of death?" (Romans 7:24). And, overcome with guilt like David, we will call out, "Restore to me the joy of your salvation and grant me a willing spirit, to sustain me" (Psalm 51:12).

2. Search out and understand what God's Word says on the subject.

What does the Bible really say about premarital sex? Can you quote the chapters and verses? How about bitterness? Or abortion? Or wife abuse? Or alcohol addiction? Or racial prejudice? Or lust? Or greed? Or jealousy? Or unresolved anger? Or genetic engineering? Or euthanasia?

Don't just ask someone to tell you what the Bible says. Don't merely read a book on the subject. Read *the* book. Search the concordance and the texts. If you struggle, ask several mature Christians to point you toward Scriptures relating to the subject.

Taking one stand at a time, become an expert at explaining your biblical position.

3. Make sincere confession of any area in your life that opposes biblical morality.

Some things that need to be changed will be old habits that have nagged you for years. You haven't spoken to your mother-in-law for five years, since she announced at the Thanksgiving dinner that her son had probably made a real mistake in marrying you. You've known all along that you should try to reconcile that relationship.

Other discoveries will be in areas you've never considered particularly offensive to God. Late-night television was just a time to relax and unwind with. OK, you argue, some of the programming is risqué—even sexually graphic—but there's nothing harmful about that. Or is there?

When you find out, confess your deviation from God's standards.

4. Pledge yourself before God to change your behavior—with the help of the Holy Spirit—one specific step at a time.

You don't remodel every room in the house at the same time if you plan on living in the home until the changes are done. What if you tackled one moral issue a month? Study. Talk. Read. Pray. Listen. Change your way of thinking. Change your way of acting.

One a month.

Twelve changes a year.

In ten years of being a Christian you would have 120 points of biblical morality to which your are solidly committed.

Without ever seeking such a status, you would be a spiritual giant.

5. Seek out a Christian friend or two who will constantly encourage you to live a godly life.

The quest to build a biblically moral life is a journey more easily completed with a friend. One who loves the Lord and is also seeking to please Him. One who can hold your secret struggles in utmost trust. One who readily admits to failures and successes. One who is looking after your best interests even as you look after his or hers. One who will meet with you once a week (or is it once a month? Or once a day?) and pray with you concerning your hassles on the road to godliness.

"Though one may be overpowered, two can defend themselves. A cord of three strands is not quickly broken" (Ecclesiastes 4:12).

Recently I read of a famous professor who spoke on some of the outdated morals of the Bible. It seems he especially did not like the scriptural teaching on the organizational structure of the home, the Bible's position on capital punishment, and the teaching restricting sexual activity to marriage.

When asked if he was a Christian, he replied, "Yes, but not in the narrow sense."

That's too bad.

Matthew 7:14 states, "Small is the gate and narrow the road that leads to life, and only a few find it."

Biblical morality is purposely narrow.

Yet that doesn't mean it is difficult to find. Anyone who has a Bible within reach has the potential for knowing what is right and what is wrong. To refuse to accept biblical standards is to actively oppose God.

To remain in the dark about the demands of biblical morality is nothing short of disregarding God's wisdom.

And nothing short of His just anger will follow.

Living the Word

It builds good relationships

1. Since we are sinful and separated from God anyway (Romans 3:23), and Jesus came to save sinful people like us (Romans 5:8), why should we bother living biblically moral lives? Give three reasons. *The sake of self esteem, sanity.*

It pays big dividends / Biblical morality has a lasting positive effe

2. Study 2 Samuel 11. What obvious moral sins did David commit? Should David have known that these things

sexual, deceitfulness, lust

were wrong? How would he have known? We know that at other times David acted as a godly man, so speculate for a moment, how do you think David justified his behavior in his own mind? Have you ever used similar arguments to justify your own behavior? When and why?

3. Now scan 2 Samuel 12–14. What three tragedies came into David's life because of this rebellion against God's morality? What does that tell you about God's position concerning our immorality?

4. If you received a personal telegram (or a fax) from the Lord, and its contents were James 1:21, "Get rid of all moral filth and the evil that is so prevalent and humbly accept the word planted in you, which can save you," would you know the particular activity(ies) in your life that prompted the note to be sent?

5. You might like to make Psalm 51:1–4 your prayer:

Have mercy on me, O God, according to your unfailing love; according to your great compassion blot out my transgressions. Wash away all my iniquity and cleanse me from my sin. For I know my transgressions, and my sin is always before me. Against you, you only, have I sinned and done what is evil in your sight, so that you are proved right when you speak and justified when you judge.

Chapter 6

A Coach's Dream

It was one of those pre-game interviews that you tolerate while you wait for the football game to begin on television. The quarterback on one of the teams is a consensus All-American and a leading candidate for the coveted Heisman trophy which goes to the best college football player in the country.

So they visited with the young man's football coach to get a little background.

"How does he get along with the other players?"

"He's an instant team leader," the coach reported. "He gives them everything he has on every play. The other guys respect that. It makes them try harder."

"What about his grades, coach?"

"Well, he's carrying a serious academic schedule, so I guess a 3.2 average is not bad, is it? He's a smart kid."

"Does he, kind of, do his own thing? Or does he pretty much follow your instruction?"

"Are you kidding?" the coach reported. "I tell him something once; he does it. That's it. No lip, no talk, no question, no need to repeat. In four years he's never been late for practice, let alone miss one. He's the first on the field, and the last to pack it up and leave. He's never broken a training rule or even tried to stretch them."

"Coach, you've got three daughters; would you want them to marry a kid like this?"

"I hope, I pray, that they can find a guy like this! Look, I figure you get a kid like this about once in your career. He's a coach's dream."

A coach's dream.

I wonder how many "coach's dreams" the Lord has on His team?

Which way do you respond when God asks you to do something?

1. *I'll see if I can work it in.*

"I appreciate the invitation, Lord. I'll go home tonight and talk it over with my spouse and kids. If we don't have any other plans, we can probably work something out."

2. *Avoiding the prison sentence.*

"Oh, Lord, not again! Nine years as a junior-high Sunday school teacher is enough to last anyone's lifetime. I've served my time, surely it's someone else's turn!"

3. *Not right now, but let's do lunch, sometime.*

"Yeah, Lord, I'll do it for you. Of course, You do realize, don't You, that I'm real busy right now? But don't worry, I've got You down on my yearly calendar."

4. *Dozing off in the spiritual fog.*

"Huh? Did You say something?"

5. *Tell Him anything just to get Him off your back.*

"Sure, Lord, I'll have it done by noon. Don't worry another minute about it. I can handle this one myself; no big deal. You know you can count on me whenever You're in a jam. I mean, have I ever let You down? Well, You know, recently? Other than those times, of course."

6. *Sorry, You dialed the wrong number.*

"Who, me? You don't mean me, do You? This is a joke, right? Are You sure You don't have me mixed up with someone else?"

7. *What are my other choices?*

"You want me to do what? I don't think that's my strength, Lord. Now, I believe I do have the gift of giving. So if You wanted to really bless me with money—maybe win the lottery, for instance—I'd be happy to use my gifts for sincere causes."

8. *Have You got anything a little more, up-front?*

"Lord, to tell you the truth, I do my best work in front of huge crowds. That's just the way You made me. So, I think I'd better take a pass on this and wait for something, You know, that utilizes my full potential."

9. *Sorry, I only work with saints.*

"To be honest Lord, well, the others in this deal are pretty shallow in their commitment. We just don't hit it off very well, so I think it's probably best to avoid getting all tangled up in that again. I'm sure You understand."

10. *The coach's dream.*

"Lord, I'm kind of scared, but I'll do it because You asked me to. I can't do it on my own. But with Your help and encouragement I'll give it my best. Thanks for Your vote of confidence."

How do you respond to God's call?

Take a look at what happened to Moses.

Born in Egypt, raised by Pharaoh's daughter, Moses fled to the wilderness after slaying an Egyptian. He was a shepherd for the next forty years. We are given no hints or indications from the scriptural record that Moses was looking for a new line of work. As far as we know he presumed that his lot in life had been settled. At age eighty, one usually does not plot out a new career. But that was just when God issued Moses His call to service. The account of that divine summons can be found in Exodus 3 and 4.

The Call of Moses

• Moses received a special revelation from God. The bush burned, yet it was not consumed. Moses was not searching for something to do, but responding to an extraordinary event. He was called by name, "Moses! Moses!" (Exodus 3:4).

- God explained to him the needs that He was concerned with. He had heard the pleas of the sons of Israel. He knew of their hard labor and misery. He knew that the children of Abraham had entered Egypt according to His leading years before. Now it was time for His plan of deliverance to begin (Exodus 3:7–8).

- Moses would have an important role in this action. He was assigned a job (Exodus 3:10). The job fit his skills, his background providing the court skills and mastery of language that would be needed. Moses might even have had some inkling of his future role years before when he intervened for a Hebrew against an Egyptian (Exodus 2:12). He was to be God's chosen instrument to lead the people out of Egypt.

- Moses responded with a protest of inadequacy (Exodus 3:11). He had fled Egypt for fear of his life (Exodus 2:15). He was not anxious to return and face the consequences of his past. Besides, his fellow Hebrews had rebuffed his earlier assistance. "Who made you ruler and judge over us?" (Exodus 2:14).

- The Lord reassured Moses. He would not be alone in the task. God had no intention of allowing Moses to try to accomplish such a thing with mere human intellect and power. "I will be with you," the Lord God announced (Exodus 3:12). What else would anyone need?

- But, to reassure Moses, God promised a confirming sign. He was to bring the Hebrew people to this very mountain, and the confirmation would be given (Exodus 3:12).

- Moses has his doubts. Not about the Lord God, but about the people. He didn't think he'd ever get them to follow him as far as that mountain (Exodus 3:13). He said, in effect, "The people won't listen to me. Who am I? Besides, I don't even know Your name. Who will I tell them sent me?"

- God understood Moses' fears. He is willing to give him what he requested. For the first time in the history of the universe God revealed what name He would like people to use when they speak of Him. Translated it means "I am who I am" (Exodus 3:14)—*YHWH* in the Hebrew, *Jehovah* in English.

• God had it all planned. Verses 15 through 22 give the details of how Moses was to accomplish that task. He would work through the elders. He was told their destination and the joys waiting for them at the new homeland. The Lord assured Moses of the value of the venture. He explained to the bewildered shepherd the process of leaving Egypt, the miracles to be performed, the stubbornness of Pharaoh's heart, and how the Egyptians would finally be glad to share their wealth with the departing Hebrews.

• Again Moses protested (Exodus 4:1). "What if they do not believe me or listen to me and say, 'The LORD did not appear to you'?"

• God, still acting with patience, performed two miracles to give the doubting Moses some assurance (Exodus 4:2ff). A staff was turned into a snake, and back to a staff again. Leprosy was given, then removed.

• Moses continued to protest. He claimed that he didn't have the qualities needed for the job (Exodus 4:10). He just wasn't the leader type, and his public speaking was pathetic. Forty years of talking to nothing but sheep had limited his social skills, or so he thought.

• God's patience began to wear thin. He firmly reminded Moses that He knew exactly what Moses' strengths and weaknesses were (Exodus 4:11–12). He was the creator of Moses, and He hadn't made any mistake—either with creation or with the divine call.

• Moses then rejected the call of God. He said, in effect, "I'm not the right person for this role, get someone else" (Exodus 4:13). This was the fifth time he had griped about God's call.

• At that point God was more than impatient, more than annoyed, more than frustrated. God was angry! (Exodus

4:14). "Then the LORD's anger burned against Moses." In seeming disgust, He turned to Moses and said something like, "You don't think I can help you be an effective speaker? Look, here comes your brother, Aaron; everyone knows how well he can speak. He can be your spokesman. I'll tell you what to do, and you can have Aaron tell the others." It was time to get on with God's plan. He had no intention of arguing with Moses any longer. Aaron was brought into the picture.

Was Moses a coach's dream?

Hardly.

God had to get angry with Moses to get him to do what He wanted. Like a child who never obeys unless there is shouting, threats, and waving of the hands, Moses protested obedience until he saw, not the fire in the bush, but the fire in God's eyes.

To drag one's feet when called to serve makes God justly angry. You can imagine how much more upset He is when we refuse His call altogether.

"Sterling is one of the leaders of the church," I was told as I began my pastorate. They were wrong. Sterling was *the* leader of the church. At first, that was quite acceptable. I needed all the help and advice I could get. The more willing lay workers, the better. In fact, that's the best way to grow a church.

But, it didn't take long for Sterling's "chats" to become tiresome events. He felt like he needed to makes the decisions on everything from janitor's hours to what color the bulletin paper should be. He gave constant advice on what themes I should preach on, which ones to avoid, which hymns to sing, and what the youth group was or wasn't allowed to do on church property.

I finally figured out that Sterling was what is known in ministerial circles as a "frustrated preacher." I should have recognized the symptoms the first time we were alone for dinner. That's when he told me his life story.

The Surprising Side of Grace

Sterling was converted to Christ in a mountain bunker in Korea at the height of the war. That foxhole conversion was real. He had a hunger to study the Bible and learn more about God. When he returned to the United States he moved to Chicago and entered Bible school. After the first year, he became convinced the Lord wanted him to preach. He and his friends would often go out to the rural areas of Minnesota and the Dakotas on preaching missions. One of the girls at Bible school helped him land a summer job at her father's hardware store in her hometown. By the end of that first summer he was in love with the young lady.

When Bible school began again, his attention was divided between his studies and his future bride. Lillian had stayed home to care for her ailing father. Right after Christmas, Lillian's father suffered a stroke that left him partially paralyzed. Sterling decided to quit school, marry Lillian, and take over her father's business. He's been a successful hardware store owner ever since.

Yet something keeps gnawing at Sterling. "I could have been a preacher, you know," he often says. His exposure to Bible school makes him, in his eyes, a theological expert. He is the one person in the congregation qualified to critique every sermon, question every pastor, give advice on every program. Any pastor who does not have Sterling on his side is not long for the pulpit of that church. He sees it as his role in life.

Actually, I believe Sterling is a gifted leader and sincere Christian. The truth of the matter is that he saw the burning bush, was called by name, and refused to go.

Cheryl has been planning to be a missionary longer than anyone I know. During her senior year in high school she attended a summer camp where the emphasis was on missions. She responded to an invitation to give her life to some type of missionary work. She prayed that God would give her a burden for a particular country.

During the school year, her best friend's family hosted a foreign exchange student from El Salvador. As they became acquainted, Cheryl felt more and more interested in the spiritual needs of that country.

She checked with mission agencies. She wrote to missionaries. She became somewhat of a expert on the politics and culture of the country. She plotted her course. It would take four years of college, then two years of intensive language study, and one additional year in Bible school. Then there would be six months of missionary boot camp, and about the same length of time to raise financial support. She figured by the age of twenty-five she would be right there in El Salvador, serving the Lord.

At the end of her senior year in college, Cheryl received a letter from Maria, the foreign exchange student she had met in high school. A small group of Christians in El Salvador was trying to start a Christian school. They needed an English teacher. This class was very important because many parents would send their children to the school for this main purpose. Maria asked Cheryl if she could possibly come down and help them get started.

"We don't need an expert. We just need someone to love the children, tell them about Jesus, and teach them how to say 'How do I get to the mall?' "

Cheryl declined the opportunity. "I haven't completed my training," she explained.

Cheryl is now thirty-four years old and she still hasn't completed her training. She became convinced that she needed her master's in Latin American History as well as a doctorate in intracultural studies, "Besides," she explains, "that's a closed field right now, what with all the political unrest and civil war. Americans seem to be the prime target. Why, that little school I almost went to has been bombed at least three times. The Lord really kept me from that situation, didn't He?"

Did He?

The Surprising Side of Grace

The other night I heard Cheryl mention to a visitor at church that she was training to be a missionary.

"What field are you interested in?" he asked.

"Well, lately," Cheryl replied, "I've been investigating the Ukraine. Of course, that will mean more language studies and stuff. But I'm willing to do whatever it takes."

Rachael is still searching for her burning bush. She had an opportunity to teach at the preschool at church, but she decided God wanted her to be a writer instead. After a $1,300 correspondence course, sixteen writer's conferences, and 100 rejection slips she's abandoned that idea.

Rachael began a ministry to shut-ins that included a meal, some housework help, and a Bible lesson. But she abandoned that to practice with several others forming a Christian music group. Their "tour" ended with only three stops. After the third performance she got into an argument with the lead singer and quit.

Rachael landed a job as secretary to the Pastor of Family Life, but quit after eight months to begin a business of being a freelance publicist and agent for Christian authors and speakers. She set up a nice office in her home, but due to circumstances beyond her control (so she reports), she has no clients.

Sometimes Rachael muses aloud about her contention that she's still searching to discover God's plan for her life.

Maybe she already has.

"Pastor, I want to start that home Bible study program I've been talking about organizing for years." Frank visited with me from his hospital bed in the cardiac care unit of the hospital.

Ever since I had come to the church, Frank had promised to get this needed program going. But leaders needed to be trained. Money had to be raised. The committee chairmen changed. Then there were vacations, business deals, and now, the heart attack.

"I've been doin' a lot of thinking," Frank continued. "The Lord showed me that if I had died, my life would not have added up to much. As soon as I'm on my feet again, I'll start that program."

He did, too. Six home Bible studies the first year. Ten the second. He has even bigger plans for the future. Did God bring the heart attack into Frank's life on purpose? I can't say, but He certainly used it to motivate a reluctant servant.

Many of us have problems similar to that of Moses. He just did not know how to say yes to God. We have all heard of Isaiah's eager "Here am I. Send me!" (Isaiah 6:8). But when we are plunked down in a real-life situation, few are so enthusiastic. We volunteer in general, then deny God the specifics.

"I have decided to follow Jesus," we sing. But when He outlines a particular course, we balk.

"If Jesus goes with me I'll go."

Well, maybe I'll go.

It's time we learned how to say an unqualified yes to our Lord and Master.

How to Say Yes to God's Call

1. Let God initiate the proposal and stir your desire.

Moses didn't rub two sticks together to get the bush burning. Nor did he douse it with lamp oil. We've got to allow God to strike the flint.

Of course, God does not use the same means for every person. There may not be any wilderness where you live, let alone bushes to burn. But your call can be just as vivid to your senses. The thought and desire to serve the Lord in a particular way will not fade away. It will spiritually burn in your bones.

After writing thirty books, I had folks ask me how I became a writer. I didn't seek it. I had no training. As far as anyone knew, I did not have a lot of natural talent to write.

But what I did have was a never diminishing ache to communicate God's truth to a larger group than my local congregation. It was that fire that drove me to attempt writing articles and stories for magazines—a desire that propelled into writing books—and it's that same compulsion that shoves me out of bed every morning at 4:20 and the same incentive that puts me behind the computer screen almost every day of the year.

But that's my burning bush. Others—even others called to be writers—will have different experiences. No matter what the details, it will be the Lord who initiates the situation and stirs up your desire.

2. Check out the scriptural validity of this particular ministry.

Paul warned us that Satan "masquerades as an angel of light" (2 Corinthians 11:14). It's possible for us to have received a "prank" spiritual call. Here are three quick guidelines.

• Your service for God must have a biblical base. God never calls us to that which is contrary to His Word. Recently a self-proclaimed prophet in the Northwest came to the media's attention. His calling was to summon Christians to rebuild their marriages to God's biblical pattern.

That sounded noble at first.

Then I found out that the pattern was based on his unique interpretation of Scripture. When he discovered a wife who would follow his advice while her husband wouldn't, he strongly insisted that the wife divorce the husband. Reports are that dozens of marriages have been ruined by following this so-called prophet. When some complained to him about the damage he was doing, he replied, "Look, sometimes we have to tear a building down and rebuild it right. That's my calling!"

Maybe he is called. But not by God.

Concerning the union of husband and wife, Jesus said, "What God has joined together, let man not separate" (Matthew 19:6).

Our calling must be biblical.

• The means of carrying out the service God has called you to must also be biblical. The method must be in harmony with the things Jesus did, or in line with the things you can easily imagine Jesus doing. He certainly desired that people "repent and believe the good news!" (Mark 1:15). But can you imagine Jesus holding a gun to someone's head and forcing them to say they've repented?

Of course not.

Jesus healed the sick (Mark 1:31, for example). But would Jesus have said, "First you must make a sizeable contribution to my ministry, then I will pray for your healing?"

Nope.

A God-given task can only be completed in a God-given way.

• The service God has called you to will fit into His kingdom plans. The world is headed toward a very definite conclusion. The whole universe, as we know it, is involved. Certain things need to happen. Our calling will fit into the big picture of the kingdom in some manner.

For example, God's plan includes sharing the gospel. The good news of Jesus Christ must be taken to all peoples (Mark 16:15). God's plan is for those who believe to grow to full maturity in Christ (Ephesians 4:13). God desires that we learn how to give love to and receive love from one another (1 John 4:7). Every valid calling will have its place in the total scope of what God wants to accomplish.

Some time ago, while speaking at a conference, a twenty-five-year-old man came up to me after the meeting and excitedly shared with me his ministry. "God has called me to tell the churches that Christ is going to return in October of 1994, and that Bill Clinton's the antichrist." I've never seen a man more serious. He asked if I would allow him to stand in front of the group and make this pronouncement.

I told him no.

I'm not in a position to cast judgment on everyone's calling, but I knew that God had not asked me to relinquish my position for this purpose. For the life of me, I couldn't figure out how that message (unbiblical as it was) could work to further God's revealed purposes in this world.

3. Commit the whole matter to the Lord in a season of prayer.

I like that word, *season*. Contrary to the calendar prediction, seasons do not begin on the same day every year. They start when the weather changes. They end when the next weather pattern begins.

How long should you pray about God's call?

For a season.

That might be different for each person, but it does indicate a substantial measure of time and effort. During that time of prayer it is quite acceptable to agree with God that you are unworthy of the job, perhaps even unskilled. Let your lack of confidence be the motivation for relying totally on His help and power. Then there comes a time to quit asking Him if it is really His will. If your heart still burns to accomplish this God-given task, then ask Him, instead, if He will show you any reason why it is not His will for you to do this.

Spend plenty of time waiting and watching for His reply.

4. Get going.

It's time to put the call into action. Begin the ministry cheerfully, wholeheartedly, as unto the Lord. Give it everything you've got. Push on to the end. Use each gift, talent, or ability you possess to see the job through, while depending every moment on the work of the Holy Spirit in your life.

Some ministries take a lifetime to complete. Some, only an afternoon.

Some acts of Christian service can alter a whole life-style. Others can be done with ease.

Some callings produce immediate results. Others will always have the conclusion hidden.

Some ministries yield instant rewards. But others have to wait until heaven for enjoyment of the prize.

There are no insignificant ministries or callings in God's kingdom. The Christian's calling is not a sentence passed down by a demanding judge, but a task given to His child by a loving Father. That's why persistent reluctance to follow His call, or out-and-out refusal to take up one's task, is such a serious matter in God's eyes.

Our reluctance proves that we do not understand the privilege of being chosen to serve God Almighty. Our reluctance proves that we do not understand the power of God to accomplish His will through our feeble efforts. Our reluctance proves that we do not understand the plan of God for His children to accomplish His goal for the entire universe.

And our reluctance to follow God's calling proves that we know very little about His loving anger.

Living the Word

1. What type of service to God really burns in your heart? How long have you had the desire to do this? Search the Scriptures and find ten Bible verses that would guide a person who had this calling.

2. Ask five mature Christian friends, whose opinions you trust, to pray with you for a season about whether this is to be your ministry or not.

3. Study 1 Corinthians 12:14–27. What does this passage tell you about the place of your particular calling in relationship to the entire body of Christ?

4. Read and memorize Romans 11:29. What does this verse mean to you personally as you consider what it is God wants you to do for Him?

5. Study Paul's review of his calling in Ephesians 3:7–21. How does Paul describe his vocation? In what way does he evaluate his skill in this area? How do you know that he understands his place in God's larger plan?

6. You might like to make Psalm 90:16–17 your prayer:

> *May your deeds be shown to your servants, your splendor to their children. May the favor of the LORD our God rest upon us; establish the work of our hands for us—yes, establish the work of our hands.*

Chapter 7

Good Pastor/Bad Pastor

Good Pastor

Lots of folks believe that the perfect pastor should be:

• Godly—a person of deep personal commitment to the Lord, one who spends much time in prayer, and gives over the details of his daily life to God.

• Dynamic—one whom others respect and follow, one who commands attention with his words, actions, and wisdom.

• Fair—one who is honest and just, who can be counted on to be consistent in seeking what is spiritually correct.

• Decisive—one who can examine all the facts of a matter and make a timely decision based on divine wisdom and common sense, then instigate a plan of action.

• Knowledgeable—knowing what is going on in the world, but, more importantly, what is going on with God's plan.

• Humble—a person who always holds a proper estimation of self, someone who is not swayed by the praise or criticism of others, but who knows his standing before God and relies on Him constantly.

• Bold—someone who holds strong biblical convictions and will stand up for them.

• Spirit-led—one in whom the Spirit of God obviously lives, as evidenced by the fruit of his life's ministry.

To discover such a candidate would thrill many a Pastor Search Committee. They would exclaim, "If we could only

The Surprising Side of Grace

find someone like that, our troubles would be over! Why, with that kind of person we would never hear another complaint about our pastor again!"

Wrong.

It doesn't work that way. Such a person would still have critics. Look at Moses, for instance. He came very close to fitting this description. Yet, he constantly faced the criticism of his leadership, even from those closest to him.

We see his brother, Aaron, and his sister, Miriam, attack him in Numbers 12. They accuse Moses of assuming that he is the only one who can know God's will. They claim he is spiritually arrogant. Surely either one of them should have equal authority.

This is a serious charge. Every leader, no matter how small the flock, must continually examine his or her motives and attitudes. Personal power can corrupt. Isolated from external accountability, a leader can assume false infallibility. God can become nothing more than one's personal crystal ball.

At first glance, there seems to be some substance in the complaint against Moses. After all, Miriam was a prophetess of God (Exodus 15:20). She had, at such times, been given God's word to speak forth. And God spoke to Aaron as well as to Moses (Numbers 4:1). But in the wilderness Moses often gave unilateral directives. He did not bring his decisions before the council of Miriam and Aaron.

Moses, alone, was called into the divine presence for special instructions. When he received the commandments from the very finger of God, Aaron and Miriam were left behind. In addition, the complaints hold little weight once the true motives of the two are exposed. In fact, their charge of spiritual arrogance is quickly dealt with. "Now Moses was a very humble man, more humble than anyone else on the face of the earth" (Numbers 12:3).

A humble man is one who has a proper view of his own abilities, one who thinks soberly of his own position.

If anything, the Bible indicates that Moses' problem was in not thinking enough of himself. So why did these two trump up charges and attack him?

The true issue had nothing to do with leadership ability, humility, theology, morals, finances, or song selection. It was a personality clash. They didn't like Mrs. Moses. "Miriam and Aaron began to talk against Moses because of his Cushite wife, for he had married a Cushite" (Numbers 12:1).

Moses had to flee from Egypt as a young man. He worked as a shepherd for the Midianite Jethro. He married Jethro's daughter, Zipporah. She apparently died, and Moses then married a Cushite—either an Ethiopian or a woman from the Persian Gulf area. Miriam and Aaron never got around to accepting her into the family.

But they committed more than a social blunder. It was a spiritual blunder as well. God answered them, "Why then were you not afraid to speak against my servant Moses?" (Numbers 12:8). It should be a spiritually scary business to criticize God's servant.

Just how angry was God?

"The anger of the LORD burned against them, and he left them" (Numbers 12:9). Only the direct intervention of Moses himself could restore them to their previous condition (Numbers 12:13).

The Lord was not implying that a spiritual leader should never be criticized. But He did make it clear that such action should not be entered into lightly. Caution should be used when questioning God's chosen leadership.

A friend of mine was asked to leave the church he was serving. One of the disgruntled members told me that the pastor "just didn't fit in."

First, his wife refused to sing in the church choir. Though she had a lovely voice, she insisted on taking a college class on choir practice nights. Then, the pastor did not get around to visiting all the shut-ins and rest-home residents members once a week (nearly thirty members fit this category). Some of his sermons dealt with controversial topics (such as AIDS, abortion, remarriage, and homelessness).

Then, the pastor did not stress one particular eschatological view often enough. Besides that, he used a different translation of the Bible than most of the board members. His sons did not seem eager to attend every church event. His car was too big, too new, and too fancy for a preacher. And, what seemed to be worst of all, he always asked for a cost-of-living raise.

Never once in all the discussion did I hear that he was anything less than godly, dynamic, fair, decisive, knowledgeable, humble, bold, and led by God's Spirit. I heard no comments about his being unbiblical. Yet, this church was not afraid to speak against God's servant.

So I asked the man, "When you called him to be pastor, was the church convinced that this was God's man for the position?"

"Well, yeah, sure, but," he stammered.

"So I presume you believe that God changed His mind?"

"I'm afraid we made a mistake back then," he rationalized.

"With that kind of record, aren't you afraid you might be making a mistake now?" I pressed.

The discussion ended rather abruptly. He did not understand my concern, nor the possibility of God's anger.

Why Pastors Are Often Wrongly Criticized

1. *Partisanship.* "He's not like Dr. Gillespie," she said. Dr. Gillespie served as pastor of First Church for twenty years. That was during the Depression. His sainthood grows with each passing year. To many, the church has been sliding downhill ever since. Lots of church members have a vision of the golden years. For them, the present pastor can't measure up to the legendary figure who once held the pulpit.

2. *Despotism.* "He'd better do as we ask. After all, he does work for us." This thought slips into even the most spiritual of minds. Some see the pastor as merely an employee, hired to do the members' bidding. It's a strange organization—423 bosses and only one employee.

3. *Jealousy.* The frustrated preachers in the congregation attack, secretly desiring a sense of power and/or fame they perceive comes with the pastor's role. They would like the benefits of spiritual leadership without the burden of the responsibilities, work, training, and divine call.

4. *Sin.* Sometimes criticism of the pastor is a smoke screen to avoid responsibility for having to listen to what the preacher has to say about unconfessed sin. They figure to keep the attention on the failures of the pastor, rather than their own unbiblical behavior.

5. *Celebrityism.* "He's sure not as good as those fellows on television and radio!" Some think the local pastor should preach, pray, sing, raise money, smile, and comb his hair like the ministers in the media. "Why isn't our worship as lively as it is on channel 40?"

6. *Vengeance.* It's a way to get even for a supposed slight or imagined rebuff. Never mind who was right or wrong. Never mind that you might have misunderstood. Never mind what pressures he was under. "I didn't like the tone of his voice at the Outreach Committee meeting last week!" So now it's time to strike back.

7. *Personal comfort.* "If I don't like the preacher, I don't have to go to church." Henry has not been to church in nearly seven years. He had a run-in with the preacher. Not even Henry can remember the exact details. Now he's in the habit of going to swap meets every Sunday. He claims he will come back when they get a new preacher. Meanwhile he figures he has an open license to criticize the present one.

8. *Guilt.* These folks think the pastor should do all those spiritual things that they never get around to doing.

"He doesn't visit my mother at the rest home often enough" usually means "I don't visit my mother enough and the pastor needs to help make up for my failure. That's what we pay him for."

9. *Depression.* "I'm mad at God, and this is my way to get even." Some tough times, some seemingly unfair consequences, some tragedies strike, and people get angry. But God is too far away and unapproachable to vent their emotions. Besides, something warns us that it's not right to be angry with God. So some decide to pick on His closest representative. They get mad at the pastor.

10. *Superiority.* "The Holy Spirit told me that my cousin from Des Moines should be our next pastor." Or, "What kind of degree is an M.Div. anyway? Surely my two Ph.D.s qualify me to pass judgment!"

But we are all painfully aware that pastors aren't perfect. Even when a man is biblically correct with his doctrine and practice, he can alienate you from his leadership. So, what can you do if you find that you and the pastor don't get along?

Pray that God will deal directly with your pastor. God disciplines his undershepherds. Moses acted rashly just once (Numbers 20:1–13), and God forbade him ever to enter the Promised Land. Even his begging God for a small taste of the land of milk and honey brought God's rebuke. " 'That is enough,' the LORD said. 'Do not speak to me anymore about this matter' " (Deuteronomy 3:26). God's judgment of His chosen servants is strict. Perhaps that is why James said, "Not many of you should presume to be teachers, my brothers, because you know that we who teach will be judged more strictly" (James 3:1).

Pray that the Lord will prevent you from becoming a public accuser of the pastor. The role of accuser of the brethren has already been assigned. In speaking of Satan, the Bible reports that "the accuser of our brothers, who accuses them before our God day and night, has been hurled down" (Revelation 12:10). Your pastor already has a very proficient accuser. The devil doesn't need your help.

Pray through Colossians 1:9–12 on a regular basis for your pastor. "Since the day we heard about you, we have not stopped praying for you and asking God to fill you with the knowledge of his will through all spiritual wisdom and understanding. And we pray this in order that you may live a life worthy of the Lord and may please him in every way: bearing fruit in every good work, growing in the knowledge of God, being strengthened with all power according to his glorious might so that you may have great endurance and patience, and joyfully giving thanks to the Father, who has qualified you to share in the inheritance of the saints in the kingdom of light."

Every congregation should wholeheartedly seek God's will when choosing a new pastor. When that one comes, forget whether he wears blue jeans or blue tuxedos, Italian loafers or cowboy boots. What does it matter if he can play softball or the concert cello? Once you have God's chosen leader, you can work together to fulfill God's unique plan for your church.

A church ministry must be built around the particular gifts, talents, and ministries of the pastor and the individual members of that body. Recognize the things the pastor does well. Then, allow him the freedom to do them. Look to God to provide others to fill in your pastor's weak areas.

Pledge yourself to do everything within your power to enable the ministry of your church to run smoothly. Murmuring, complaining, and protesting about God's chosen leadership is dangerous business. Approach it only when you are willing to contend with an angry God.

Bad Pastor

OK, what about false leaders? What about pastors involved in sin? What about those who choose to deviate from biblical teaching. It does happen, doesn't it?

105

Yep.

What does God think about such pastors?

" 'Woe to the shepherds who are destroying and scattering the sheep of my pasture!' declares the LORD" (Jeremiah 23:1).

Is God really angry at this situation?

"The anger of the LORD will not turn back until he fully accomplishes the purposes of his heart" (Jeremiah 23:20).

How do you know if a pastor has fallen into this despicable condition? Here are several things to consider:

• False leaders speak out of their own minds, rather than expounding God's Word (Jeremiah 14:14). Their doctrine has little or no scriptural foundation. They feel no compulsion to base their sermons on the Bible. The theme of their messages will be guided more by what is politically correct or what people's "itching ears want to hear" (2 Timothy 4:3), rather than the central themes of God's truth.

• False leaders will tell of spurious visions and dreams. (Jeremiah 23:31–32). There will be tales of angels revealing new doctrine, life-after-death experiences that contradict Bible teaching, visions that bring profit to the leader.

• False leaders can be deceptive in appearance (Matthew 7:25; 2 Corinthians 11:15). Their looks, manners, language, and actions will, at first, seem quite orthodox.

• The problem of false leaders will grow more prevalent as the day of the Lord's return approaches (Matthew 24:11).

• False leaders can have miraculous ministries (Matthew 24:24). True miracles of God should cause much rejoicing. But miracles alone should never be the single factor in validating a ministry.

• False leaders can become very popular. "The prophets prophesy lies, the priests rule by their own authority, and my people love it this way. But what will you do in the end?" (Jeremiah 5:31).

• False leaders are of no value in God's kingdom. " 'They do not benefit these people in the least,' declares the LORD" (Jeremiah 23:32).

• False leaders are most often motivated by greed (Jeremiah 6:13; 1 Timothy 6:5). They want money, power, fame, or even sexual gratification. The result of their work is destruction of the flock. "I know that after I leave, savage wolves will come in among you and will not spare the flock" (Acts 20:29).

• False leaders can rise up from the very membership of a church. "Even from your own number men will arise and distort the truth in order to draw away disciples after them" (Acts 20:30).

• False leaders will sometimes follow demonic leading. "Some will abandon the faith and follow deceiving spirits and things taught by demons" (1 Timothy 4:1).

• False leaders will set up arbitrary, unbiblical rules and force everyone to follow them (1 Timothy 4:2–5).

• False leaders deviate from the clear teaching of Jesus Himself. "If anyone teaches false doctrines and does not agree to the sound instruction of our Lord Jesus Christ and to godly teaching, he is conceited and understands nothing" (1 Timothy 6:3–4).

• False leaders focus on the trivial and unessential. "He has an unhealthy interest in controversies and arguments that result in envy, quarreling, malicious talk, evil suspicions and constant friction . . ." (1 Timothy 6:4).

Actually, the biblical list of warnings about false leaders could go on and on. From Moses, to Jeremiah, to Paul, to the present, worthless shepherds have appeared among God's flock trying to lead them away. The problem has always been how to tell the good ones from the bad? How do we know whom to believe? Here are four signs:

1. Every shepherd worth following must lead a godly life.

Samuel is a glowing Old Testament example of this principle. When he retired from the office of priest, prophet, and judge, he said that he had been faithful to God since he was a child. Then he asked all the people of Israel to make public any offense he may have committed against anyone. Not one person stepped forward with a complaint. I don't think he was trying to brag. I believe he really wanted to be reconciled (1 Samuel 12:1–5).

John the Baptist was another who lived out what he preached. Jesus said of him, "I tell you the truth: Among those born of women there has not risen anyone greater than John the Baptist" (Matthew 11:11). Not Abraham. Not Moses. Not David. Not even Samuel could supersede John. Herod may not have liked all of John's preaching, but he could not say a word against the way he lived his life (Mark 6:18–20).

Even Paul, formerly a persecutor of Christians, began to live a godly life upon conversion. He was so confident of the way he lived that he did not hesitate to encourage people to pattern their lives after his (1 Corinthians 11:1; Philippians 4:9).

Samuel, John, Paul—those men were listened to, not just because of what they said, but because of their actions. Any modern Christian leader caught up in sin does not deserve to be believed or followed.

2. Every shepherd worth following must teach biblical doctrine.

Paul sets the standard in Titus 1:9 when he says, "He must hold firmly to the trustworthy message as it has been taught, so that he can encourage others by sound doctrine and refute those who oppose it."

Some believe that since no two people agree on every minute detail of biblical interpretation, everyone should be left to himself to determine matters of doctrine. But orthodoxy is not impossible to define. Dixon, Torrey, Meyer, Warfield, Ryle, Morgan, Scofield, Gray, Pierson, and the others who established the fundamentals early in the twentieth century did a good job of spelling out the essentials of the faith.

Here are the kinds of doctrinal questions you have a right to ask everyone seeking a position of Christian leadership in your church.

• What is God like? What are His attributes? How does He reveal Himself to be? Explain to me the Trinity. What does it mean to call God "Father"?

• What does it mean that the Bible is God's inspired Word? How about inerrancy? How did we decide which books should be included in the Bible? Are some books more valid than others?

• Tell me about Jesus' deity. His humanity. His place in creation. His incarnation. His death for me. His relationship to the Father and the Holy Spirit. His role in my life now. His place in heaven. His role in the future.

• How about the Holy Spirit? Who is He? Where is He? What does He do? How is He involved in salvation? Does He dwell in all believers? How can I be filled with the Spirit?

• Tell me about the spirit world. What are angels? Demons? What do they do? What about Satan? Just how powerful is he? In what way does he attack believers?

• What does the Bible say about humankind? What's the character of man without Christ? How did sin get into our world? Just how sinful are we?

• What does it mean to be saved? How does it come about? What is election? What are the benefits of salvation? What's Jesus' role in my salvation? Just how secure am I in my salvation?

• What is the church? How should it be governed? What are the ordinances of the church? How did the church begin? How will it be completed? What is it supposed to do on this earth?

• How about the end-times? What happens then? When does Christ return? What does He do when He comes back? Who gets judged, and when? What about heaven and hell? Tell me about the millennial kingdom. Who will make it to heaven?

Now, to some, all this sounds like an inquisition. If you're on a pastor-seeking committee it's a pretty fair outline to follow during one of the interview sessions. Other than that, don't plan on smothering any person with all these questions at once. But it gives you the idea of the kinds of questions you have a right to ask.

All answers should come with biblical support, and there should be a willingness to deal with all the texts on the issue, not just selected ones.

3. Every shepherd worth following must exhibit heavenly wisdom.

Wisdom is using the best possible godly methods to achieve the best possible godly results. James 3:13–18 describes the difference between earthly (unspiritual) wisdom and that which comes from heaven.

Characteristics of True Wisdom

• Pure—cleansed of all ulterior motives.

• Peace-loving—pursues right relationships between God and humanity, and between people.

• Considerate—the ability to back off, even if one is right, in order to produce even better results.

• Submissive—a willingness to listen to the other side of the question; approachableness; knowing when to yield.

• Mercy and good fruit—sympathy for one in trouble, even if it's his own fault he's in trouble; sympathy that produces practical help.

• Impartial—fair without wavering, not hesitant or vacillating in judgment or support.

• Sincere—never acting out a part that one does not truly believe in.

4. Every shepherd worth following must produce righteous fruit.

Look at the results. Although this is not an absolute indication of a teacher's orthodoxy, results that a ministry produces can be instructive. Some folks should be finding a personal relationship with Jesus Christ through this ministry. Believers should be maturing in their faith. Some attempt should be made to meet the needs of the poor. Those oppressed by Satan should be set free. The true words of our Lord should be clearly proclaimed. Believers should be trained and equipped to do their unique ministries. Jesus Christ should be honored by receiving glory for all accomplishments. Satan's strongholds should show signs of defeat. In other words, God is at work in this ministry! "Peacemakers who sow in peace raise a harvest of righteousness" (James 3:18).

Another guide would be to look for evidence of the fruit of the Spirit. Results of a true ministry will produce "love, joy, peace, patience, kindness, goodness, faithfulness, gentleness and self-control" in the lives of believers (Galatians 5:22–23).

To be a shepherd of the Lord's flock is a majestic and dreadful calling. To lead the sheep astray is to tread on most dangerous ground. But even in the early church some dared to do so.

In Corinth some thought there was no resurrection (1 Corinthians 15). Galatian teachers emphasized legalism and Judaism (Galatians 3:1–5). Some in Philippi proposed lawlessness which led to self-indulgence and immorality (Philippians 3:17–21). Those at Colosse were proponents of a misguided view of Christ (Colossians 1:15–20). Peter warned of those who encouraged immorality and rebellion (2 Peter 2).

The solution is to find a balance between submission to God's appointed leadership and cautiously rejecting false shepherds. The following is meant to be a helpful guide, but it must be used with discretion, grace, compassion, and the leading of the Holy Spirit.

How to Criticize the Shepherd

1. Examine your motives. Do you have genuine love and concern for your pastor as a person? Offering advice should not be motivated to gain power, prestige, or pleasure for yourself.

2. Look for confirmation. OK, you've noticed something that you feel is wrong; does the Bible confirm your suspicions? Do other spiritually mature believers agree with your evaluation? Did they come to that position without your prodding?

3. Approach the pastor with the right attitude. Assume that there is an explanation for this particular behavior or teaching emphasis. There is always the possibility that you and your friends have misunderstood the situation.

4. Discuss your concerns privately. At this point do not broadcast public commentaries. Explain what has been troubling you with a careful presentation of how you interpret the biblical guidelines.

5. Allow the Holy Spirit to convict. It is not your role to pressure the pastor into your point of view. Clearly present your case, then let it rest. Determine to pray daily for the one you confronted.

6. Offer a reasonable alternative. Don't just condemn what is wrong without suggesting what is right. Counsel a way to overcome the problem. Your purpose is to build a stronger ministry, not to destroy one.

7. Be ready to give your full support. The effort to change may require help from others. Be willing to volunteer to assist in making things right.

8. Provide sufficient time for change. The length of time needed to correct the situation depends on the offense involved. An immoral relationship must be severed instantly. An incorrect doctrine may take weeks and months of study to overcome.

9. Follow the guidelines of Matthew 18:15–17 and 1 Timothy 5:19–20 if your private efforts are futile. Your

next visit must be with the aid of several mature and sensitive church leaders. If this fails, the subject should be brought before the entire congregation.

10. Love the offender no matter what. Don't stop caring if this person refuses to comply with your request. False or erring spiritual leaders are people, too. They should not be treated as robots of deception.

11. Exclude this one from the fellowship, if that time comes. If the conduct or doctrine continues to prove to be apostate, and the person involved shows no willingness to change, the Lord's instruction is to oust him (1 Corinthians 5). This is an extreme case and requires much loving, prayerful caution.

12. Give the glory to God if the leader does respond. Only the Holy Spirit can cause one to accept criticism and repent of his or her ways. You should stand in awe that God allowed you to be used as an assistant in such a holy calling, remembering that the day could come when it is you who needs the correction.

There could be a time when you sadly discover that your shepherd is indeed false. After you have done all that you were allowed to do to carry out the hope of restoration, to no avail, there might be nothing left to do but leave the fellowship and look for a shepherd who is faithful and true.

Good pastors.

Bad pastors.

God knows the difference.

The good ones are close to His heart. Attack them, and you invite a confrontation with the anger of God.

The bad ones already stand condemned. They have violated the sacred trust of God's calling. They will, without fail, taste His anger.

That is sufficient.

Living the Word

1. Read Acts 6:4. From this verse what would you say is the main ministry of the pastor? Do you think your pastor has been given enough time to successfully complete this part of the ministry? If not, how can you help see that he does?

2. Study 2 Peter 2. What are the characteristics of false teachers here? What is God's attitude toward them? What will their future be?

3. Look at Acts 18:23–28. Who corrected Apollos's theological errors? What method did they use to do this? What was the result?

4. Read out loud 1 Timothy 5:17–18. It's talking about a pastor's wages. What does it say they should be in relationship to the average wage in your congregation? Does your pastor's salary reflect this guideline?

5. You might like to make Psalm 20:1–5 your prayer for your pastor:

> *May the LORD answer you when you are in distress; may the name of the God of Jacob protect you. May he send you help from the sanctuary and grant you support from Zion. May he remember all your sacrifices and accept your burnt offerings. May he give you the desire of your heart and make all your plans succeed. We will shout for joy when you are victorious and will lift up our banners in the name of our God. May the LORD grant all your requests.*

Chapter 8

What Do We Deserve?

"Well, they certainly don't preach sermons like they used to!" Mrs. Alcott reported.

"Eh, I, eh, suppose they don't," I mumbled for the fifty-second consecutive week.

"We aren't giving enough to missions!" she continued without relinquishing my hand.

"No, ma'am," I offered. "We would like to do better in that."

"The sanctuary was too cold; I had to wear my sweater and it's only September," she continued, blocking the main exit of the church after the Sunday morning service.

"Perhaps if you sat away from the door, the draft wouldn't be as bad," I counseled gently.

"I've sat in that pew for sixty-one years, I don't intend to move. It's, it's a family tradition. I remember sitting right there and coming to church with my mother and father—now those were the days! That's when this church was really alive!"

I finally ushered Mrs. Alcott out the front door and turned to greet the other worshipers.

Every pastor has days like that.

For me it was once a week for six years. Every Sunday morning. Without fail.

You just can't please some folks. Anyway, that's the way it seems. Mrs. Alcott was one of those people that I hated to ask, "How's everything going?" She had complaints against me, the church, the community, the neighbors, and God. "Good morning, Mrs. Alcott," usually brought an argument.

As I got to know her better, I realized the underlying current of her pessimism had to do with her resentment against God. She was a widow. Why did God have to take her husband so soon? She was left with oversight of a ranch operation, but she didn't see that as support for her old age. She rarely acknowledged her good fortune in having two grown sons nearby to help out, because her daughter (who lived 2,000 miles away) didn't visit often enough. The weather was too warm. Or was it too wet? Or dry? They had to irrigate too often. Her bad knee was always acting up. Her blood pressure was high ("under too much stress," I was told). I got the feeling that Mrs. Alcott thought God had shortchanged her.

Linda is always depressed, too. To listen to her you would believe she's hopelessly caught in a spider's web of negative circumstances. "What did I do to deserve this?" she asks. She keeps searching for God to give her an answer that instantly cures all her dilemmas.

Linda's twenty-eight, married to a Christian man, and has three active children. Her husband, Ron, is a policeman, with an erratic work schedule. She worries constantly about his safety. And she's alone a lot of the time with little Susan and the twins. Three children in thirteen months have her in a permanent stage of exhaustion. Her days consist of diapers, feedings, washings, and rocking cranky little ones.

Her master's degree is still six units and a thesis away. She hasn't played the piano in months, and she has no idea 'where in the world her oils and brushes are. She's still driving the used compact car she bought to take to college (the one whose driver's door never seems to close!). She hasn't had enough grocery money to buy a roast since last Easter.

"What am I doing wrong?" she asked me in tears. "I'm trying to do things God's way; I just don't know why something couldn't go right!" she moans.

Sometimes, Linda feels like God is punishing her.

In the tough job of being a mother of little ones, on a limited budget, Linda's forgotten a few things—her Christian husband, three healthy children, a warm comfortable home, a loving family living in the same city, a church home, and a Lord and Savior who's promised to be with her every moment of her life.

Richard came back from his twentieth college reunion dejected. During those years at school he had developed a goal for how he would own his own business by the time he was thirty, and be able to retire at fifty. His senior paper spelled out the goals and objectives. It was the top paper in the class.

By thirty-one, Richard owned the Kid's Choice Toy Store. At age thirty-six, he filed for bankruptcy. Now he's forty-three, working for average wages—scraping by with the help of his wife's salary and a home loan from her parents.

"Charley McReynolds was there at the reunion! Drunk as always. Some blonde about twenty-one hanging all over him. He's got thirty-seven video stores now—rolling in dough. I don't understand!" Richard laments. "Charley's been married four times and indicted once. Me? I've towed the line every day of my life, and what has it got me?"

Peace with God, and an eternity with Jesus, for starters. But Richard doesn't always see that.

Ingratitude.

Like a small weed seed it grows and strangles the very joy and abundance out of life.

The wilderness of the Sinai Peninsula is bleak and barren. There is an occasional oasis, but mainly it is rocky,

117

timberless, dead desert. It must have been quite a contrast to the moist, fertile, green, and humid Nile River Valley of Egypt. The Israelites following Moses worried about survival. Six hundred thousand mouths were a lot to feed. The logistics of the problem were overwhelming. But God handled the situation simply. He invented a new food: manna.

Each morning a fine flake-like substance fell to the ground, a miraculous residue of the evaporating dew. All the people had to do was gather enough for the day's meals. Any more than that was forbidden. God had a lesson to teach. He wanted them to learn to trust and rely upon Him. On the day before the Sabbath they could gather two days' supply so they would have a day of rest.

The miniature flakes were ground, then boiled or baked into a type of bread. It was truly a miracle food. All the daily requirements for vitamins and nutrients were provided. But, of course, the people soon whined.

They wanted meat. They wanted fish. They longed for the cucumbers, melons, leeks, onions, and garlic of Egypt. They were willing to trade their newfound freedom for their former slavery, just for the pleasures of a varied diet. The simple lifestyle on the road to the Promised Land did not appeal to them.

So, what did God think of their ingratitude?

"The LORD became exceedingly angry" (Numbers 11:10).

Could it be any more clear than that?

The people's attitude greatly dishonored their Lord God. They were showing that they did not believe Him to be all-knowing. They clamored for God to come and see what was going on. Apparently they figured He was off somewhere and was not keeping a careful watch on their situation.

They ignored the fact that God's understanding is infinite, that He is well able to see the past, present, and future at all times. He not only knew the people's actions, He knew their inner thoughts and motives, too. He cared what happened to them. Surely all He had taken them through proved that.

If they accepted the fact that God knew about their predicament and that He cared for them, then their complaints must have stemmed from the assumption that God was powerless to help. It was impossible to have meat out there in the desert, so they thought.

They were saying, in effect, "either God doesn't care about us, or He's not powerful enough to do anything about it." In doing so, they had just mocked God's integrity and His strength. No wonder He was righteously angry.

If it had not been against His very nature to do so, what would it have been like if God had given in to their gripes and allowed them to return to Egypt? Would they have returned to slavery, a policy of infanticide, and hard labor, with increased persecutions and hatred because of the plagues and sorrows dealt the Egyptians by the Israelite God?

They would also have had to face a continual state of living in rebellion against God. They were the ones who had called for help in Egypt. Now they were spurning that assistance. How long would it have been before He ever listened to their pleas again? What a terrible thing to be abandoned to their own resources! What would their life had been like if God had just given up on them?

Paul gives us a little glimpse of that kind of life that is governed by one's own decisions.

"Since they did not think it worthwhile to retain the knowledge of God, he gave them over to a depraved mind, to do what ought not to be done. They have become filled with every kind of wickedness, evil, greed and depravity. They are full of envy, murder, strife, deceit and malice. They are gossips, slanderers, God-haters, insolent, arrogant

119

and boastful; they invent ways of doing evil; they disobey their parents; they are senseless, faithless, heartless, ruthless" (Romans 1:28–31).

If God had granted their request to return to Egypt, they would have missed out on His best for their lives. No Promised Land flowing with milk and honey. No great and glorious Hebrew kingdom. No future Messiah from among them. No central place in the history of the world. They would have remained a forgotten group of slaves who would, sooner or later, have been consumed by another nation and known only, if at all, to some future archaeologists.

Are the leeks and garlics really that valuable? What is worth the price of stepping out of God's will? Our always present complaints indicate a willingness to forfeit all God has planned for us. We think we have a clear idea exactly what we're giving up in order to follow Christ. Do we have just as clear a view of what we forfeit if we could exchange our walk in God's will for the things in this world? Only then can we truly evaluate whether we are getting the best end of the bargain.

We have something in common with the wandering Hebrew nation. We, too, are "aliens and strangers in the world" (1 Peter 2:11) in this land. We, too, have a great many blessings and benefits that are offered to us from God's mercy and grace.

Yet with all of this, and more, we also can slip into a lifestyle of ingratitude. Here's a self-test that might help you see yourself more clearly.

• Are most people "better off" than you are?

• Do you often think or say, "no one has to go through what I do!"?

• If you were given three wishes, would you immediately change the circumstances around you?

• Do you often find yourself praying, "Lord, this just isn't fair!"

• Do you seriously believe that you would be just as well off right now (or even better off) if you had never come to Christ?

• What three subject matters have dominated your mind most during the past week? Have they centered around what you are missing? Or what you have received?

• Fill in the blank, "If only God would _____." Was that easy to complete? Did you have many items to list?

• How do you respond to the statement, "Life is one long pain to be endured in order to escape the wrath of hell"?

• Is it true that "God blesses some, more than others?" Why did you answer that way?

• On a scale of one (zip, nada, nothing) to ten (incredible!) how blessed are you?

Sometimes, in the loneliness, hurt, anger, and selfishness we cry out that we deserve better than what God is giving us.

So, perhaps, we need to review from time to time what it is we really deserve from God.

What Do We Deserve?

"All have sinned and fall short of the glory of God" (Romans 3:23).

"The wages of sin is death, but the gift of God is eternal life in Christ Jesus our Lord" (Romans 6:23).

"What benefit did you reap at that time from the things you are now ashamed of? Those things result in death!" (Romans 6:21).

"Every living soul belongs to me, the father as well as the son—both alike belong to me. The soul who sins is the one who will die" (Ezekiel 18:4).

"Although they know God's righteous decree that those who do such things deserve death, they not only continue to do these very things but also approve of those who practice them" (Romans 1:32).

"When we were controlled by the sinful nature, the sinful passions aroused by the law were at work in our bodies, so that we bore fruit for death" (Romans 7:5).

"The mind of sinful man is death" (Romans 8:6).

"If you live according to the sinful nature, you will die" (Romans 8:13).

"After desire has conceived, it gives birth to sin; and sin, when it is full-grown, gives birth to death" (James 1:15).

The verses go on and on, but even a Bible novice can understand that picture.

What do we all deserve?

Death.

And that is the just fate that awaits us. But, in the meantime, God, in His love, chooses to send us blessings and opportunities.

What Has God Done for Us lately?

1. He provides all our natural resources.

"He causes his sun to rise on the evil and the good, and sends rain on the righteous and unrighteous" (Matthew 5:45).

2. He provides for our daily necessities.

"Do not worry, saying, 'What shall we eat?' or 'What shall we drink?' or 'What shall we wear?' For the pagans run after all these things, and your heavenly Father knows that you need them" (Matthew 6:31–32).

3. He provides us with families.

"Sons are a heritage from the LORD, children a reward from him" (Psalm 127:3).

4. He provides us an opportunity for salvation.

"God demonstrates his own love for us in this: While we were still sinners, Christ died for us" (Romans 5:8).

5. He provides us with a life of abundance. "I have come that they may have life, and have it to the full" (John 10:10).

6. He provides us with the highest quality of life imaginable.

"The fruit of the Spirit is love, joy, peace, patience, kindness, goodness, faithfulness, gentleness and self-control" (Galatians 5:22–23).

7. He provides a purpose and direction in life.

"He rewards those who earnestly seek him" (Hebrews 11:6).

"Store up for yourselves treasures in heaven, where moth and rust do not destroy, and where thieves do not break in and steal" (Matthew 6:20).

8. He provides us a personal divine helper in our struggles of life.

"The Counselor, the Holy Spirit, whom the Father will send in my name, will teach you all things and will remind you of everything I have said to you" (John 14:26).

9. He provides us with an eternal dwelling place.

"In my Father's house are many rooms, if it were not so, I would have told you. I am going there to prepare a place for you. And if I go and prepare a place for you, I will come back and take you to be with me that you also may be where I am" (John 14:2–3).

10. In fact, He provides us with more blessings than we can ever comprehend.

"Praise be to the God and Father of our Lord Jesus Christ, who has blessed us in the heavenly realms with every spiritual blessing in Christ" (Ephesians 1:3).

"Now to him who is able to do immeasurably more than all we ask or imagine, according to his power that is at work within us . . ." (Ephesians 3:20).

I recently attended a birthday party for an eight-year-old daughter of a friend of mine. The candles were blown out, the cake was cut, and the presents opened. She ripped her way into dolls, dresses, games, books, and stuffed animals.

One present came from Grandma Grisham. She lives in Corsicana, Texas, and hadn't seen her granddaughter for a couple of years. It was a small flat box and Carrie didn't hide her expectation of getting a video game from Grandma.

The package was wrapped in plain brown paper, and the card was one that Grandma Grisham had made herself. Inside, was a very small hand-beaded purse with a leather shoulder strap.

"A purse?" Carrie moaned. "What do I need a purse for?" The brightly colored little handbag was tossed over into the pile of discarded ribbons and paper. It was Carrie's mother who retrieved the purse in order to survey her own mother's handiwork. After opening the little purse, she handed it back to her daughter.

"Carrie," she instructed, "you'd better look at Grandma Grisham's present again."

"It's just a purse," Carrie pouted.

"But it's a special purse. Grandma made it just for you. Did you see the way she spelled out your name in the beads?"

"Oh, cool," Carrie nodded. "Would you hand me that big blue present?"

"Carrie," her mother scolded, "if I were you, I'd look inside your new purse."

Her daughter nonchalantly flipped open the little purse and stared inside. Faking a faint, Carrie fell off her chair to the carpet with a squeal.

"I don't believe it! Is it real? Is it mine?"

Grandma Grisham had tucked a crisp $100 bill inside the purse.

Carrie almost missed it. Disappointed by what she perceived to be an inferior gift, she nearly missed the quality craftsmanship and the surprise inside.

Later, when Grandma Grisham called, it would have been a tragedy for Carrie not to have even noticed the monetary gift and therefore offer no thanks.

After the party Carrie's mom told me, "I don't know why my mother does that; she can't afford to give away that much money! She's just getting by on her Social Security check, you know."

Well, I know why she does it.

She loves Carrie with a love so deep it approaches unreasonability. She misses her granddaughter and wants to be with her. She's hoping that Carrie remembers her. She prays that there will be a day when they can spend time together.

So she sacrifices, without reservation.

And so does our heavenly Father.

You and I are not eight-year-olds.

And the wallet has a whole lot more than a $100 bill.

No wonder our constant ingratitude stirs His anger.

It's a marvel that's He's put up with some of us this long.

Living the Word

1. List ten of your positive qualities. Take time. Ask others if you want. Then draw a line through every one that was given to you by God. (Include looks, personality, temperament, spiritual gifts, ministries, etc.) Next, cross out those that were produced by your God-given environment as you grew up (learned from family, neighbors, church, community, etc.). Then eliminate those positive qualities that came into your life by following biblical principles (honesty, morality, truthfulness, etc.). OK, what do you have left? Did God have any part in these qualities that are left? Then scratch them off. Now, what you have left are your self-made attributes.

2. Now, list ten of your most important accomplishments in life. Subtract those that came about with God's help. That includes any assistance from friends, family, outside material resources, since all of that comes from God also.

3. Review those two lists. Jot down five things you deserve from God that He has withheld from you unfairly. Write down the reasons why you believe God should honor each of your requests.

4. If you feel that you just might have demonstrated too much ingratitude and not enough thanks, confess it now to your heavenly Father who loves you dearly.

5. You might want to make Psalm 145:3–7 your prayer:

> *Great is the LORD and most worthy of praise; his greatness no one can fathom. One generation will commend your works to another; they will tell of your mighty acts. They will speak of the glorious splendor of your majesty, and I will meditate on your wonderful works. They will tell of the power of your awesome works, and I will proclaim your great deeds. They will celebrate your abundant goodness and joyfully sing of your righteousness.*

Chapter 9

Love Without Obedience/
Obedience Without Love

Pink roses decorated the front of a very pretty Mother's Day card. Inside, next to a warm greeting was signed, "I Love You Mom! Crissy."

Margo enjoyed receiving the card from her fifteen-year-old daughter. But on this particular Mother's Day Sunday it rang a little shallow.

On the previous Friday, Margo had hurried around before work and prepared her husband's favorite taco casserole. She left it in a foil-covered pan in the refrigerator. Then she carefully explained to her daughter how to put the dish in the oven and set it for 325 degrees at 4:30 p.m. "That way when we get home from work, supper will be ready," she explained to her nodding daughter. To insure that the casserole got cooked, Margo left a bright note on the kitchen counter.

When she arrived home at 5:52 p.m. she was surprised not to smell the aroma of the simmering casserole wafting throughout the kitchen. Margo was shocked to find the taco dish still in the refrigerator.

"Crissy!" she hollered through the hall.

With stereo earphones still on her head, Crissy peeked out of her room.

"Why in the world didn't you put that casserole in the oven like I asked? Did you forget? I left you a note. Surely you saw the note!"

"I remembered about the taco casserole," Crissy protested, "but, well, we had tacos for lunch today and I just wasn't hungry for the casserole."

"You what?" her mother shouted. "That was supper for all of us!"

"Hey, don't sweat it, Mom. I called out for pizza, they'll be here any minute," Crissy offered. "It'll be about $25, I guess."

"You ordered pizza? I didn't tell you to order any pizza!" Margo protested.

"Look," Crissy sighed, "I don't see what's the big deal."

Chances are a similar scene has happened at your house. The beautiful Mother's Day card would have had more impact if the love was backed up with obedience. It's sometimes difficult to believe someone else cares much about you if they are continually disregarding your instruction.

Our disappointment and anger over what we perceive to be insensitive, inconsiderate rebellion seems quite justifiable.

Did you ever wonder how God feels when we disregard His instruction?

Imagine a country in which there existed only one Bible. That Bible was kept in a huge church in the nation's capital. The church taught from that one Bible to all the people of the land.

Now, suppose those church leaders grew tired of their teaching chores. With time the unused Bible was stored in a musty room in a far corner of the building. Oh, worship services continued. Offerings were still taken. God was still mentioned. But His written Word was ignored. Then years, decades, even generations passed. The congregation eventually did not even know that a Bible existed. They still held to forms of worship, but the forms lacked meaning.

Then, suppose the great church at the nation's capital began a restoration project. The decrepit building needed repair. The new leader desired to renovate the original architectural beauty. And while his workers rummaged through the storage rooms, they found a book. After glancing at it carefully, they realized its importance. They then brought the book to the leader and it was read to him in its entirety. He was astounded at what he heard.

The leader humbled himself before God, asked forgiveness for their neglect of His book, and pledged to obey every part of it. God forgave and exalted the leader to an important place in His kingdom. All because of reverence for God's written Word.

A fairy tale?

Nope.

It happened just that way according to 2 Kings 22 and 23. While His Word was being ignored, what was God's mood? According to that king, Josiah, "Great is the LORD's anger that burns against us because our fathers have not obeyed the words of this book; they have not acted in accordance with all that is written there concerning us" (2 Kings 22:13).

When His instructions are discarded, God is rightfully angry.

But why would people, in any age, purposely ignore God's Word to us?

Why People Don't Obey the Bible

1. Some people don't believe it.

The Bible is described by some to be an ancient Middle-Eastern document that is good only for discovering a few facts about early Hebrew culture and primitive religious thought. Other critics are not so refined.

As I waited for my check in a restaurant, I began to read my pocket New Testament. "Are you reading a Bible?" the man next to me asked.

"Why, yes," I replied, "I read it often. How about you?"

"Nope. Not me. You won't catch me reading the Bible."

"Why's that?"

"It's full of lies, that's why!" he reported.

"Oh?" I quizzed, "What do you mean?"

"To begin with, it claims the world was created by God in seven days. That can't be. The earth took billions of years to evolve. We all know that. Then it says that dead people can be raised to life. That's not true. I've never seen it happen, have you? Then Bible says God is love, but thousands of innocent babies die every year. I tell you, it's full of lies. You'd be just as well off reading what I read."

"What's that?" I asked.

"Science fiction. Say, did you know they now have proof that there's life on Venus?"

2. Some people don't understand it.

Paul said that for some "The god of this age has blinded the minds of unbelievers, so that they cannot see the light of the gospel of the glory of Christ, who is the image of God"

(2 Corinthians 4:4).

Jim caught me by the arm in the courtyard of the church and blurted out, "Did you know that all the demons are going to be saved?"

"Wh–, what?" I choked.

"Yeah, it says so right there in James 2:19 that the demons believe. Yes, sir, I read it this morning."

"But, Jim," I explained, "that only means that even the demons realize that God exists. That's not the same thing as trusting in Christ as their Lord and Savior."

"Well," he huffed, "that's not the way I read it. After all, I'm sure God wouldn't want anyone to go to hell, right?"

Jim was wrong.

But thirty more minutes of explanation failed to convince him. Some folks disobey God's Word because they seem to be blinded to its truth.

3. Some people don't know what it says.

Many otherwise sincere Christians are very close to being biblically illiterate. Sometimes it's because they aren't in a church that faithfully teaches and preaches the Word. Sometimes it's their own neglect.

Three of Bob's coworkers sat with him during the lunch break. The topic turned to gay rights in the military. "Hey, Bob," one of them said. "You're a Christian. What does the Bible really say about homosexuality?"

"Oh, well, it's against it, I'm sure it's against homosexuality," he stammered.

"But, I mean, specifically. Where would a guy read to find out about it?" the man insisted.

Bob had to admit he just wasn't sure. He would have shown them the chapters and verses, if he had known any.

What does the Bible say about assisting suicides? About remarriages? About abortion? About tithing? About capital punishment? About violating a union contract and going out on strike, anyway? About sexual harassment in the workplace? About genetic engineering? About birth control?

There are times when we find ourselves disobedient to God's Word simply because we don't know what it really says about the subject.

4. Some people don't think it's all meant to be obeyed.

"This is the most practical book I own," Harry told me as he thumped the huge family Bible sitting on the coffee table. "Yep, whenever I run across something I can't handle I just leaf through the Bible and get comfort from its words."

Then, I suppose trying to impress me with his devotion, he continued.

"Why, I even underline the parts that still apply to us today."

The parts that still apply?

I presume that Harry underlined every verse. But, of course, he didn't. In fact, as I glanced through the pages of Matthew I could see very few verses underlined.

The Surprising Side of Grace

Harry was working with an abbreviated Bible. Obeying only the sections that he wanted to obey.

5. Some people don't take the Bible literally.

There are times when we read the Bible through special intellectual filters. Every statement can be explained away by certain modern interpretations. "God does not really mean what He says He means," we insist.

For instance, when Matthew 5:4 says, "Give to the one who asks you, and do not turn away from the one who wants to borrow from you," we insist that doesn't mean Tony, the next door neighbor who never brings tools back, or the transient down at the truck stop.

When Jesus says, "Anyone who says, 'You fool!' will be in danger of the fire of hell" (Matthew 5:22), some folks are convinced that Jesus doesn't really mean fiery hell. Instead, they insist, that just means life will be uncomfortable here on earth.

Or, when Jesus says, "If anyone would come after me, he must deny himself and take up his cross and follow me" (Matthew 16:24). He certainly isn't insisting on radical obedience, rather He just wants to make sure we are actualizing our full potential.

But what God means is exactly what He said. His Word doesn't need to be reinterpreted, it needs to be obeyed.

6. Some people don't believe the Bible was given in their best interest.

"The Bible's too narrow!"

"I'll miss all the exciting things in life, if I try to follow the Scriptures!"

"My situation is unique, I don't think it fits the Bible pattern."

"Man, if I tried to do everything the Bible wants me to do, it would be like being in prison!"

In reality it's just the opposite. Jesus said, "If you hold to my teaching, you are really my disciples. Then you will know the truth, and the truth will set you free" (John 8:31–32).

Just how good are those excuses for not obeying God's Word?

Suppose you're driving down one of those long, straight, flat highways of northern Nevada. Not a car, not a house, not a living thing can be seen for miles. At least, so you think. All of a sudden, a flashing light reflects from your rear view mirror. A Nevada state police officer wants you to pull over.

You look at your speedometer. It points to 75 miles per hour. When the officer walks up to your car, which of the following excuses will you give?

• "Well, I saw the 55 mph sign back there, but it was so old and rusted I thought surely that wasn't the speed limit anymore."

• "Officer, that sign doesn't have anything to do with speed. It means 55 <u>M</u>iles to the <u>P</u>almer <u>H</u>ouse cafe."

• "55 mph? Why, I didn't know that!"

• "As a general rule, I do drive 55, but this was one exception. Nobody should be expected to drive 55 all the time!"

• "Look, officer, that sign meant 55ish. You know, give or take a little. Some miles back I was stuck behind a truck going 35, so I'm just making up the difference."

• "The law is absolutely absurd! Here I am, out in the boonies wanting to hurry home, and you say I ought to drive slow enough to change tires? It isn't fair!"

Now just how impressed and convinced will the officer be with any of those replies?

Well, God isn't too impressed with our disobedience either.

Here's why. First John 5:3 states "This is love for God: to obey his commands. And his commands are not burdensome."

One of the primary ways we can demonstrate our love for God is to obey His words. To say that we love without any corresponding actions is cheap and unconvincing.

The Surprising Side of Grace

Besides showing a lack of love for the Lord, our disobedience demonstrates lack of trust in His wisdom and lack of concern for His plan. It is, perhaps, the ultimate act of hypocrisy to claim to love God, and then ignore His commands.

Love of God without obedience to Him is shallow and meaningless.

Likewise, mechanical obedience without love for mankind or God is also of little value.

Obedience without love easily slips into legalism. God not only cares about what we do; He cares about how and why we do it.

Which of the following are examples of legalism?

• Terry sits in uniform at the airport, waiting for a ride home. He's been in Germany for two years. No one's there to meet him, but he knew it would be this way. His plane arrived on a Sunday evening, and his folks won't be out to the airport until after the service. They just couldn't miss Sunday evening church—"What would people think?"

• "You did what?"

"I bought a new vacuum cleaner," she said.

"But, how could you? You never asked me for permission!" he complained.

"I know, dear. But ours was broken, and Wanda was selling her perfectly good one at the garage sale for fifty dollars. So I bought it."

"Don't ever do anything like that again. I'm the head of the home, it says so in the Bible, and I'll make the decisions on purchases!"

• "I'm never going back to that church again! Did you hear that music? And all that shouting? Can you imagine a guitar and drums in a Sunday morning service? The Bible plainly says we should worship decently and in order. Well, that certainly didn't measure up!"

• "I'm really worried about the type of people we're letting join our church. You know that fellow Rawlins? We understand that he smokes! And not only that, his wife used to work in a bar!"

• "Dear Brother Kline, I can see by the records that you and your wife are several months behind on your 'Double-Tithe Love Offering.' I just wanted you to know that two weeks from Sunday will be the day we bring all the names of Tardy Tithers before the Lord during the morning worship services. I'm sure it is your wish, as it is mine, that your names do not appear on that list."

Which one is legalism?

They all are. Sometimes it's very subtle. Other times it's obvious and blatant. Legalism is excessive conformity to one's personal interpretation of the law, often without regard to the needs and feelings of others. Seldom does the Bible condemn anyone who desires to apply legalistic standards to his or her own life. But it does condemn those who try to force those rules on others. The religious leaders of Jesus' day were quick to try and force Him into their legalistic system. Starting with a biblical premise, "Remember the Sabbath day by keeping it holy" (Exodus 20:8), they had spent years building an elaborate system of rules about what could and couldn't be done on the Sabbath.

Their plan was to catch Jesus in public breaking one of the rules, expose His error and thereby invalidate (so they thought) His whole ministry.

In Mark, chapter 3, they set the trap. At the synagogue where Jesus is present, they bring a man with a birth defect, a shriveled hand. The plot was simple: place the man up front. Jesus, whom they knew was a pushover for needy people, would heal the man. Doctors were not supposed to practice their profession on the Sabbath because that was work, and work was forbidden. It was all right to keep yourself or others from getting worse on the Sabbath, but you couldn't do anything to make them better.

Jesus walked into the synagogue and immediately took charge of the situation. He said to the man, "Stand up in front of everyone" (vs. 3). At this point the Pharisees must have felt He was about to be caught in their trap. Quite the opposite was true.

"Then Jesus asked them, 'Which is lawful on the Sabbath: to do good or to do evil, to save a life or to kill?' But they remained silent" (Mark 3:4).

Now, this is not a tough question. Every person in the building knew the answer. But the Pharisees hesitated. If they gave the correct answer—it is lawful to do good, to save a life—then they would be agreeing with His action to heal the man. If they said the opposite, everyone in the room would know that they were lying. Trapped, they said nothing.

They were trying to apply their human legalistic standards to Jesus and they cared nothing for the people, or for the man with the birth defect. The Scriptures say Jesus "looked around at them in anger and, deeply distressed at their stubborn hearts, said to the man, 'Stretch out your hand' " (Mark 3:5).

Jesus was angry.

Furious.

Insensitive legalism stirs God's just anger. Too often it involves using a religious sounding excuse to absolve a person from the action and attitude God desires.

Dangers of Legalism

1. God's commands bring freedom; legalism brings bondage.

When a small child is told he can't play in the street, the rule is not meant to enslave him to the yard. It's meant to protect him from harm so that he might have many more years of play. God's commands come for our protection. Legalism not only keeps the child out of the street; it would keep him or her out the yard as well. Yards can be perilous. Soon the child is kept in a sealed, padded room, and even then the legalist is looking for more restrictions.

2. Legalism is most often based on one's personal interpretation of Scripture.

The Bible isn't legalistic.

People are.

Fred gets paid monthly. His wife would like to write one check for the church when she pays their monthly bills. Fred won't let her. "The Bible says you should give to the Lord on the first day of the week," he points out. Therefore he insists they bring an offering every Sunday. He also believes that offerings must remain secret, so he insists on a cash sum every Sunday. This means a trip to the bank every Friday of the year for his wife. He insists it's the only biblical way to give.

In this, Fred is legalistic.

3. Your interpretations of the rules of Christian life are judiciously applied to others.

Katherine never wears makeup or jewelry, nor does she braid her hair or wear expensive clothes to church. "It's against the Bible," she insists. Now, she certainly has the right to dress the way she does. But Katherine doesn't stop with her own appearance. More than one visitor has quit coming to church because Katherine has told them in a very loud voice that their dress and makeup is not appropriate for a church service.

4. Legalism can, at times, actually supplant faith.

George has been a widower for over ten years. His life is an orderly routine. Each day there is Bible reading, each Sunday two worship services, and on Wednesday, there's prayer meeting. He pays his tithe, helps with the props for the kids' choir, supports a missionary in India, and serves on a church committee. His neighbors never complain about him, and his reputation in the community is high.

George plans to keep up the routine until the day he sails right through those impearled gates of heaven. But George has a problem. He's never personally accepted

Jesus Christ as Lord and Savior. Religious routine—in this case, good religious routine—has displaced faith.

5. Legalism can sometimes replace true love and devotion to God.

If our spiritual commitment is only a matter of keeping the rules, then a daily, vital walk of love and fellowship with God is not necessary.

Obedience should flow out of a love relationship with the Lord. "We love because he first loved us" (1 John 4:19).

6. Legalism cannot sustain itself indefinitely.

No one can maintain even his or her own set of rules without occasionally failing. "If we claim to be without sin, we deceive ourselves and the truth is not in us" (1 John 1:8). An honest legalist is doomed to spend his or her life either feeling like a failure, or living in hypocrisy.

7. Legalism forgets that people are more important than rules.

God is not in the business of saving rules and Jesus did not die for the Bible's sake. God saves people. Sinful people. And those people are exactly the ones who will spend eternity with Him in heaven.

The compassion of the Lord toward people above rules is seen clearly in John 8 when He deals with the woman caught in the act of adultery. It is a hideous, life-destroying sin that she has agreed to, and Jesus doesn't not negate disobedience or its consequences. But He challenges her accusers. They care nothing at all about this woman. They care only about trapping Jesus when he fails to follow their rules.

But Jesus cares about people. So He tells her, "Go now and leave your life of sin" (John 8:11).

Legalism could never do that.

But Jesus did.

So how do we handle the balance between obeying God's Word and becoming legalistic? Here's one plan that might work for you.

1. Accept the fact that all Scripture is to be obeyed.

2. With the guidance of the Holy Spirit, apply God's Word to your everyday life.

3. Work to live consistently with your understanding of the Bible.

4. Do not arbitrarily apply your standards of behavior to other believers.

5. Meet with at least one other mature Christian to whom you can be accountable both as to how you live your life, and how you go about interpreting Scripture.

6. Have as your goal the building up of others' spiritual lives, instead of tearing them down.

Our role should be "Let us consider how we may spur one another on toward love and good deeds" (Hebrews 10:24). Satan's role is to accuse Christians "before our God day and night" (Revelation 12:10). He doesn't need our help.

God enjoys enthusiasm in obedience to His commands. But we must not become so blinded in obedience to human standards that we crush people along the way. That kind of behavior has always stirred the just anger of a loving God.

Living the Word

1. Read Zechariah 7:11–14. What generates God's anger in this passage, and what does He promise to do in response?

2. Start making a list of the five most repeated moral topics of conversation you hear at work. Use that for a study list and find out what God's Word has to say about each one.

3. Study and memorize 2 Timothy 3:16. If a person believed this verse to be true, what implications would that have for the rest of the Bible?

4. Ask three mature Christian friends if they would jot down one or two areas in which you sometimes come across as legalistic. Prayerfully consider what God would want you to do about their replies.

5. You might like to make Psalm 119:36–37 your prayer:

> *Turn my heart toward your statutes and not toward selfish gain. Turn my eyes away from worthless things; preserve my life according to your word.*

Chapter 10

Broken Promises

The Code of the West.

It never was written down. Perhaps that's because many who followed it could neither read nor write. But when you find yourself in a wild and unpredictable environment 500 miles from the nearest lawman, there had to be some order of life to keep anarchy, murder, and self-destruction in check. So the early trappers, cattlemen, and prospectors formulated the unofficial Code of the West, or the minimum behavior expected of all men.

At the top of everyone's list: Keep every promise. No man was better than his word. It mattered little to anyone what another man had been "in the states." His worth was now validated by how he kept his word.

In September of 1878 Andrew Garcia set out from Bozeman, Montana, to hunt buffalo. His string of ten pack mules and gear took every penny he had saved and then some. In fact, he was $300 short. A merchant in Bozeman gave Garcia "Jawbone-credit." Garcia promised to return and pay the money by January 1.

But the snows came early that year and Garcia was stranded in the Rockies. Finally, he began to work his way south. By spring he was in southern Colorado, and by summer, in northern New Mexico. Some cronies told him to forget the merchant up in Bozeman. "He probably thinks you're dead by now," they advised.

But Garcia headed north for the 1300-mile trek. By the time he reached Bozeman, it had been a year since his departure. He sold his hides, and paid off the merchant.

It was quite simple to Garcia.

He owed the man money. And he had promised to pay it back.

So he did.

It's the Code.

In many places, the Code of the West faded with the buffalo and Pony Express. These days it takes six attorneys to draw up intricate contracts. Even then, they're not considered absolutely binding. Contracts are scoured for loopholes. "I'll show it to you in writing" is about a meaningless as a man's word.

"I promise I'll . . . ."

Promise what?

How good is your word? Is it as good as you want it to be? How valid is your word to God?

A vow is a solemn promise or assertion by which a person binds himself to a certain act, service, or condition. In the Bible, a vow is most often used in connection with a promise made to God.

In Genesis 28, Jacob made a vow. God had given Jacob a wonderful promise, "I am with you and will watch over you wherever you go, and I will bring you back to this land. I will not leave you until I have done what I have promised you (28:15).

After that Jacob vowed, "If God will be with me and will watch over me on this journey I am taking and will give me food to eat and clothes to wear so that I return safely to my father's house, then the LORD will be my God, and this stone that I have set up as a pillar will be God's house, and of all that you give me I will give you a tenth" (Genesis 28:20–22).

It was a vow of a scared man. Fleeing from his homeland to avoid the wrath of a brother he had swindled,

Jacob fears for his life. "Get me through this God, and I promise. . . ."

Not a very noble motivation for a vow to God? Perhaps not. But God honored His promise. And Jacob kept his word.

Sometimes vows were made to God by the whole Hebrew nation. In Numbers 21:2 it records, "Then Israel made this vow to the LORD: 'If you will deliver these people into our hands, we will totally destroy their cities.' " God kept His part of the agreement, and so did the people of Israel.

Some vows recorded in the Bible were foolish. Like Jephthah's, in Judges 11:30–31, which ended up condemning his own daughter. But even then, Jephthah does not even consider breaking his promise to God.

Some vows come from a broken heart. "In bitterness of soul Hannah wept much and prayed to the LORD. And she made a vow, saying, 'O LORD Almighty, if you will only look upon your servant's misery and remember me, and not forget your servant but give her a son, then I will give him to the LORD for all the days of his life and no razor will ever be used on his head' " (1 Samuel 1:10–11). When the Lord gave her little Samuel, she dedicated him to the Lord and sent him to be raised by Eli the priest. She was a woman who kept promises.

Even in the New Testament, vows are made, and kept. Paul makes vows both in Acts 18:18 and Acts 21:23–26.

God does not take our vows lightly. He expects us to reflect His image. His word is absolutely good at all times. "God is not a man, that he should lie, nor a son of man, that he should change his mind. Does he speak and then not act? Does he promise and not fulfill?" (Numbers 23:19).

His word is absolutely, innerrantly good at all times. He speaks, and it becomes a reality. God doesn't need to cross His heart, say "I promise," or sign a contract. "No matter how many promises God has made, they are 'Yes' in Christ" (2 Corinthians 1:20). Jesus is the proof that God keeps his Word.

A vow or a promise, whether verbal, written, or uttered from the heart in silent prayer, is an opportunity for a Christian to demonstrate God's control in his life. To break that vow or promise is to demonstrate rebellion against Him. You can imagine how He responds to such actions:

"When you make a vow to God, do not delay in fulfilling it. He has no pleasure in fools; fulfill your vow. It is better not to vow than to make a vow and not fulfill it. Do not let your mouth lead you into sin. And do not protest to the temple messenger, 'My vow was a mistake.' Why should God be angry at what you say and destroy the work of your hands? Much dreaming and many words are meaningless. Therefore stand in awe of God" (Ecclesiastes 5:4–7).

Is God's anger justified over a vow repealed or a promised forgotten? Jesus said, "Simply let your 'Yes' be 'Yes,' and your 'No,' 'No'; anything beyond this comes from the evil one" (Matthew 5:37). When we say "Yes, Lord," we had better mean it. To change our mind, to break a vow, to discard a promise, is in Jesus' words "from the evil one." In other words, it's demonic.

No wonder it stirs such a response in God.

But what kind of vows do we make before the Lord? Here are a few samples.

Sacred Vows

Marriage vows

Myrna and David stood before me and several hundred guests on Saturday, July 16th, and repeated their wedding vows at the front of the flower-lined sanctuary. "I do promise and covenant; before God and these witnesses; to be thy loving and faithful husband [wife] as long as we both shall live."

We had spent six sessions together in counseling about the significance of their vows and what God would expect of that commitment.

In the second week in January I read in the newspaper that they had filed for divorce. "What happened?" I asked Myrna when I saw her later in the week.

"Oh, it wasn't your fault," she assured me. "It's just, well, it didn't work out. I guess we aren't very compatible, that's all. We gave it some time, but it wasn't getting any better, so we just backed away from it before we did anything we'd regret. I hope you aren't angry," she smiled.

I was deeply disappointed. And saddened. But they didn't make that vow just to me.

Salvation vows

Bart sat in my office with a mind full of questions about Christianity. "How do we know God exists?" "Why is Christ the only way to God?" "What do I have to give up when I become a Christian?" "Why does God let bad things happen?" "Do I have to be baptized to become a Christian?" "Will I have to give ten percent of my income to the church?" "What's all this talk about the Holy Spirit?"

He thought he might like to become a Christian, so I tried to answer each question. Then I explained how a person can come to personal knowledge of Jesus Christ. I attempted to carefully present the evidences on which our faith is based. And again there was a bank of questions.

Finally after several hours of discussion, he fell silent.

"Bart," I asked a few minutes later, "would you like to accept Christ right now?"

"Yes, I would."

"Do you have any more questions?"

"No."

With a sincere prayer, Bart confessed his sins, asking Christ to become his Lord and Savior, and vowing to follow Him all the days of his life.

I was surprised when I didn't see Bart the following Sunday in church. I called and left a message on his answering machine. But he didn't call back. When he didn't come to church the next Sunday, I stopped by where he worked.

As soon as I walked up, he blurted out, "It just didn't stick!"

"What? What didn't stick?"

"You know, that Christianity stuff. Oh, what you said was good and all. Don't take it personal, but I guess it just doesn't work for me."

I quoted to him several verses of assurance and then reminded him of his sincere prayer of confession. "You remember what you prayed, don't you?" I asked.

"Yeah, well," he stammered, "I guess I didn't really mean what I was saying."

A salvation vow that wasn't really meant? Playing around with the death of Christ on the cross for your sins? It was not a cheap vow that he broke.

Crisis vows

These can sometimes be the fastest vows in history.

Deborah's pickup truck hit a patch of black ice as she and little Jessica drove home through the mountains one night. The '90 Chevy Silverado spun three complete circles and slid toward an oncoming truck.

She later reported to me that for some reason she cried out, "Lord, if you get us out of this safe, I'll sing in the church choir!" The truck swerved. The pickup didn't roll. In fact, it came to a rest between two groves of pine trees along the highway. No injuries. No damage to the vehicle.

The next Wednesday night Deborah was in choir.

"It's kind of a dumb thing," she admitted. "I mean, I don't know why that was the promise that I made. But I figure I'd better keep it. Don't you think so?"

Church vows

Whatever happened to the Princellises?

They were the tall couple with the two little girls. They drove the red mini-van and used to sit in fourth pew on the right, next to the window. They moved to the community about a year ago, and started attending our church right away.

"Just the kind of church we've always wanted!" they bubbled enthusiastically.

Standing before our congregation with a dozen others, they promised to serve as the Lord's faithful disciples to their lives' end and support the ministry and service of this church. But Pete got elected to the school board and there seemed to be a district, regional, or state meeting about every weekend. Pauline was gone most Sundays to set up displays at craft shows, and we really haven't seen her around here in months.

Oh, they're still on our church roles. And will be forever, I suppose. What about those vows before God?

National vows

"I pledge allegiance . . ." To what? To the flag? And to the Republic? What kind of republic? "One nation, under God." There's His name again. Every time we repeat it, we are calling God to witness our commitment to the country in which He has placed us.

So what does God think when we set out to weaken or defraud the government we vowed to support? Would He be pleased that we weaseled out of jury duty? Refused to vote? Cheated on our taxes? Does He really expect us to judiciously keep that vow?

Listen to Paul, "Everyone must submit himself to the governing authorities, for there is no authority except that which God has established. The authorities that exist have been established by God. Consequently, he who rebels against the authority is rebelling against what God has instituted, and those who do so will bring judgment on themselves" (Romans 13: 1–2).

Love vows

Cindy was so enthralled with the weekend spiritual life conference at college. For three days they had studied, prayed, praised, and sung about God's glory, majesty, and power. Filled with adoration and excitement, her devotion to God was at an emotional high. Then, in the final message, she heard the most inspiring message about the need to bring the lost to God's love. She was ready to march right out of the building and off to the ends of the earth.

"Lord," she prayed silently to herself, "thanks for being so good to me! I promise I will spend my life helping the lost hear about your Son, our Savior, Jesus Christ."

A vow from a loving heart. From a child who is caught up with the glories of the Father. A promise sincerely made, even if not completely thought out.

Does such a vow please God?

I think so.

Does He really expect Cindy to keep this promise?

Yep.

Marriage vows. Salvation vows. Crisis vows. Church vows. National vows. Love vows. They're just a sample of the kinds of promises we make before God.

Since the Lord takes all vows so seriously, some suggest that it would be better if we didn't make any vows at all. Sometimes that might be the best advice. Deuteronomy 23:22 states, "If you refrain from making a vow, you will not be guilty." And Ecclesiastes 5:5 reminds us, "It is better not to vow than to make a vow and not fulfill it."

In fact, there are those who interpret Matthew 5:33–37 to claim that Christians should never make any vows at all. Jesus said, "But I tell you, Do not swear at all" (vs. 34). But what He condemns are the petty games that some people had made out of giving vows. For them, "I promise" didn't mean anything. But if they said "I promise by heaven!" or "I promise by earth!" or "I promise by Jerusalem!" or even "I promise by the gray hair on my head!" such phrases held varying degrees of validity.

They had made vows before God a game, with plenty of escape routes. Jesus exhorted them to forget all those wordy, meaningless vows. Instead, make a simple "yes" the only vow you need (verse 37).

"Yes, Lord" is a vow. And the only words we need.

But it would be good if you and I were more careful about the vows we make to the Lord. There are no unimportant promises to God. There are a few questions we need to ask ourselves before we make such an oath.

Vow Checklist

_____ 1. Is this a voluntary commitment?

"Whatever your lips utter you must be sure to do, because you made your vow freely to the LORD your God with your own mouth" (Deuteronomy 23:23).

There should be no external physical, psychological, or social pressure forcing your decision.

_____ 2. Have you considered the end to which this vow could lead you? (Remember Jephthah in Judges 11?) You are committing yourself to live with the consequences of this promise.

_____ 3. Can your part of the vow be measured? How will you know when you have completed your part? For instance, a wedding vow, pledged before God can be evaluated by demonstrating love and faithfulness "in plenty and in want, in joy and in sorrow, in sickness and in health." But it's only on our deathbed that we can say that we have kept that vow.

_____ 4. Is the vow you are about to make biblical? Does it violate the words or the spirit of the Scripture? If every Christian made such a promise, how would God's kingdom fare? Is it a biblical vow to ask, "Lord, I promise that if you let me win the $111 million lottery, I'll give ten percent of it to the church"? First Timothy 6:10 seems to indicate the foolishness of such a promise. "The love of money is a root of all kinds of evil. Some people, eager for money, have wandered from the faith and pierced themselves with many griefs."

_____ 5. Are you willing to carry it out without altering the terms of the promise? Many times we are champions of compromise and appeasement. At age eighteen we make a vow to God to give our life serving Him on a foreign mission field. When we're twenty-two we decide that domestic missions are just as valid a place to channel our energies. At age twenty-six we're sure that part-time ministry, as we continue with our vocation, will be a satisfactory response to our earlier commitment. By the time we're thirty, we've decided that supporting missions with substantial financial gift is really what the Lord wants from us. In order to do this we need a renewed commitment to make money. At age forty, we feel good about the fact we're giving a regular, moderate sum to missionaries. But, of course, with our children all in college, by the time we're fifty we've cut back to a minimum in order to help kids. But, more or less, we've kept that vow.

Or have we?

_____ 6. Are you confident you can meet the deadline you set for yourself? "If you make a vow to the LORD your God, do not be slow to pay it" (Deuteronomy 23:21). "When you make a vow to God, do not delay in fulfilling it" (Ecclesiastes 5:4).

When you and your spouse vow in September to donate $5,000 to the Lord's work by Christmas, can you do it? A vow is not a place to experiment with your discipleship. A vow is a solemn commitment that you are going to do it, no matter what.

_____ 7. Have you thought through the fact that breaking this vow could very well stir up the just anger of God?

The words of a popular television commercial taunt, "image is everything." Nothing could be further from the truth. As far as the Lord is concerned, "integrity is everything." David prays, "I know, my God, that you test the heart and are pleased with integrity. All these things have I given willingly and with honest intent" (1 Chronicles 29:17). Broken vows are a serious character flaw in God's children, they will not be leftunchallenged.

One of the best preparations for keeping our vows before God is to build a habit of keeping all our promises, no matter how small, or to whom they were made. The Lord, and those close to you, have a right to be suspicious of the person who claims to keep the big vows if they never demonstrate an ability to keep the little promises of life.

Every promise is an opportunity to practice the Godlike quality of being true to your word.

"I'll be home at 6:00."

"I'll take you shopping on Saturday."

"I promise to attend the marriage enrichment seminar."

"I'll never let the bank account get overdrawn again."

"I'll call you as soon as I get there."

"I'll play basketball with you after work today."

"We'll go to Disney World next summer."

"I'll clean the garage next Thursday."

"I'll quit watching those soap operas."

"We'll get a puppy next spring."

Promise-keeping.

It's not the only way to evaluate the seriousness of our commitment to the Lord.

But it's a mighty good place to begin.

God longs for us to be people of our word, reliable children whose promises reflect the integrity of their heavenly Father. The Code of the West was never as strong and binding as the code of Christ. And to violate His code brings more than just sagebrush justice. It's a good way to stir up His anger and discover the other side of His grace.

Living the Word

1. Study Ephesians 4:15. What's the relationship between the truthfulness of our speech and Christian maturity?

2. Read Psalm 119:106. What kind of oath did the psalmist make? How would he confirm this?

3. Now take a look at Psalm 25:21. The psalmist obviously put his hope in the Lord. What two things does he offer as collateral for such hope?

4. Ask God to bring to mind the last vow that you made to Him. If nothing comes to mind quickly, seek His response daily until you do receive an answer. Now, what have you done with that vow? If you find yourself coming up short, confess your faults and commit yourself to keep that pledge.

5. Ask each family member to jot down two or three of the last promises that you made to them. (You might have to help them understand what kinds of things you mean.) Now, gather up their reports and evaluate yourself. How are you doing at keeping your word to your family? If you discover promises that have not yet been kept, go to a calendar and record the date on which you will complete each of them.

6. You might like to make Psalm 7:8 your prayer:

> *Judge me, O LORD, according to my righteousness, according to my integrity, O Most High.*

Chapter 11

Siding With the Enemy

If you've never been called a wild-eyed, religious fanatic before, may I suggest an easy way to remedy that deficiency? Walk into your nearest mall and survey the items on shelves of the toy store. Then walk up to the cash register and proclaim in a voice loud enough for all to hear, "Did you know that you are selling demonic items to children?"

You will probably be ushered out the front door, and if you insist on continuing the conversation, mall security will be called.

The truth remains. Our society has come to accept much of the occult and demonic as harmless games, innocuous toys. Few folks take Satan seriously, and that's just the way he wants it.

Betty never missed her horoscope in the local newspaper. Every day, she grabbed up the want ads, flipped to the last page, spotted the Sagittarius paragraph, and counted the stars in the listing. (five stars mean a dynamic day, four mean positive, three mean average, two mean so-so, one means difficult).

"It's just for fun," she explains. "Some people read the advice columns, others the letters to the editor, or the comics, or the sports statistics. My thing is reading the 'scopes!"

But somewhere along the line, Betty stopped laughing at the fortune-cookie-like advice and began to believe it.

The Surprising Side of Grace

Now, she still looks like an average, middle-class suburban wife and mother. She avoids weird or bizarre behavioral changes—most of the time.

It's just that on certain days she wouldn't dare venture out of the house. Other days are good for trips. She knew just the right time to ask her husband, David, to buy her a new dress, the exact time of the month to talk to her mother-in-law, and when was the best time to transfer money from checking to the savings account.

After a year or so, Betty was dissatisfied with the tiny blurb in the paper and she began to purchase books on the subject. She became the neighborhood expert on the subject of astrology. "It's just a fun hobby," she rationalizes. "It's certainly better than watching the soaps!"

Nowadays, Betty's phone bill rockets each month with the number of calls to a 900-number psychic advisor that she saw advertised on television.

Betty seldom misses a Sunday at church; and never, ever misses her daily horoscope.

A harmless game? A fun hobby?

That's not how God would explain it.

A eighteen-year-old boy in a trance was arrested while staggering in the streets of northeast Los Angeles. The officer thought he was stoned or drunk. As it turned out they could not find any trace of drugs or alcohol in his system. But they did make a startling discovery: in his coat pocket was a human finger.

Investigation uncovered the fact that he was a member of Coven Thirteen. These Satan-worshipers met in a small storefront building on Eagle Rock Boulevard. Before this discovery, no one had taken the group seriously. "Just some punk rockers and old hippies doing their thing," most thought.

But what was really going on in that building?

Some people now wanted to know.

Others were afraid to find out.

Betty and this young man in northeast Los Angeles have something in common. The forms differ, but they're both participating in deceptive spiritism. Both could be classified as occultism, even though one seems harmless and the other grotesque. Occult practices seem to be present in every generation. The Bible is filled with examples.

Godliness is not an inherited characteristic. Hezekiah ranked as one of the better kings of Judah. Josiah, his great-grandson, just might have been the best king Judah had ever known. But in between those two ruled a couple of losers: Hezekiah's son, Manasseh, and his grandson, Amon. Under their leading, the people who were supposed to be the spiritual light to the Gentiles ("I will keep you and will make you to be a covenant for the people and a light for the Gentiles" [Isaiah 42:6]) had become a beacon of darkness.

Manasseh built idolatrous places of worship. He encouraged allegiance to Baal and Asherah, foreign gods, right in the great temple in Jerusalem. In addition, he personally delved into the occult.

"In both courts of the temple of the LORD, he built altars to all the starry hosts. He sacrificed his own son in the fire, practiced sorcery and divination, and consulted mediums and spiritists" (2 Kings 21:5–6).

God's reaction to this behavior is predictable, and probably understated in 2 Kings 21:6 when it reports that the king "did much evil in the eyes of the LORD, provoking him to anger." But this is not the only case of God's hatred of occult practices. Some of the activities recorded in the Bible that stir God's anger include:

• Magical incantations, which includes magic formulas and spells. None less than the infamous Jezebel is accused of bringing these into Israel. " 'How can there be peace,' Jehu replied, 'as long as all the idolatry and witchcraft of your mother Jezebel abound?' " (2 Kings 9:22).

155

The Surprising Side of Grace

• Good luck charms. Not rabbit's feet, but little quarter-moon trinkets. "In that day the Lord will snatch away their finery: the bangles and headbands and crescent necklaces" (Isaiah 3:18). Such "charms" could be worn on the body or placed in the home; in either case the intent was to provide protection from evil spirits.

• Chanting. Meaningless repetitions continued mindlessly until the desired result occurred. In Acts 19:34 huge crowds of residents packed into the arena and screamed in unison for two hours, "Great is Artemis of the Ephesians!" What Jesus thought of this type of action is summed up in Matthew 6:7 "When you pray, do not keep on babbling like pagans, for they think they will be heard because of their many words."

• Astrology. Attempting to predict the future by interpreting supposed signs given in the heavens. In Stephen's final sermon he stated that because the people of Israel refused to follow God's instruction and insisted they worship pagan gods, "God turned away and gave them over to the worship of the heavenly bodies" (Acts 7:42). Astrology can lead to the actual worship of the stars, planets, and moon. King Josiah is commended for doing away with "the pagan priests appointed by the kings of Judah to burn incense on the high places of the towns of Judah and on those around Jerusalem—those who burned incense to Baal, to the sun and moon, to the constellations and to all the starry hosts" (2 Kings 23:5).

• Examination of animal innards. Called hepatoscopy, this is a gross form of divination by examination of the liver of animals. Ezekiel 21:21 states that the king of Babylon, will come to a crossroad and trying to divine the right route, will "examine the liver." Many believed that the size and condition of various parts of the liver was a prediction of future success or failure.

• Tossing the arrows. Again in Ezekiel 21:21, the Babylonian king is predicted to "cast lots with arrows." It sounds a lot like tossing a coin to make your decisions. If the coin is tossed as a neutral random method of selection (such as before a football game to see who kicks off first) then the action is harmless. If the arrow, or coin, is tossed in the belief that its outcome will predict the future, then it becomes occult.

• Consulting household gods. Called teraphim, these little statues are frequently associated with divination. In Zechariah 10:2 it says, "The idols speak deceit, diviners see visions that lie; they tell dreams that are false, they give comfort in vain."

• Conferring with the dead. The calling on the dead for advice or help is an old occult practice clearly condemned by Scripture. "Do not turn to mediums or seek out spiritists, for you will be defiled by them. I am the LORD your God" (Leviticus 19:31).

The person who engages in any and all of these activities was called in the Bible a sorcerer or sorceress. The punishment for such an offense was blunt and unmistakable: "Do not allow a sorceress to live" (Exodus 22:18). In God's eyes such a person forfeited their privilege of life. It was a cancer so evil to society that only radical surgery would stop the destruction.

Why Does God Get So Angry at Occult Practices?

1. The one involved in occult activity has purposely refused to allow God to have His rightful place in guiding his or her life. To consult any other source, whether a simple good luck charm, or seeking the very person of Satan, reveals a fear of the future and a distrust in God's ability to lead and protect us. It stems from a desire to know something that God has in His wisdom chosen to keep secret. This displays a distrust in God's gracious leading and His perfect will. It is man's attempt to control his own future apart from God's wise counsel.

157

The Surprising Side of Grace

Think about Betty and her attachment to horoscopes. She once read, "Difficulties await you in making major decisions today." She felt that meant canceling a shopping trip to buy a new dress to wear to her son's wedding. In fact, she decided not to buy a new dress at all, until a clear sign was given in the horoscope. But Jesus said, "Seek first his kingdom and his righteousness, and all these things [like food and clothing] will be given to you as well. Therefore do not worry about tomorrow, for tomorrow will worry about itself. Each day has enough trouble of its own" (Matthew 6:33–34).

There is a place we can turn for everyday guidance and spiritual wisdom, but it's not found in the occult.

2. God's anger is set against those who jump into occult activity because they have lost self-control and become enslaved to forces beyond themselves. His purpose in creation is to make us so that we could freely love Him and be united with Him in fellowship forever. The dangerous trap of the occult bars us from achieving that divine purpose. All occult activities build a strong dependency, whether it is emotional, psychological, spiritual, or physical. Even well-educated people find they cannot function from day to day without direction from their occult source. This renders a person useless to benefit from God's wisdom, mercy, guidance, forgiveness, and love.

One so-called psychic counselor told Betty that he could help her in her battle to lose weight, but she would have to agree to follow his instructions exactly. To deviate, or ignore any part of his instruction would bring a curse upon her. Now she feels trapped and is too frightened to break free.

3. The most offensive part of occult activity is that the person has opened up direct communication with Satan, himself. It is a voluntary enslavement to his evil influence and power.

Until Christ's return, two sources of supernatural power exist in this world. One is the Lord God; and the other is Satan. How great is Satan's power? Paul warns, "Be strong in the Lord and in his mighty power. Put on the full armor of God so that you can take your stand against the devil's schemes. For our struggle is not against flesh and blood, but against the rulers, against the authorities, against the powers of this dark world and against the spiritual forces of evil in the heavenly realms" (Ephesians 6:10–12).

A spiritual battle rages. There are two distinct sides in the conflict. To succumb to the occult is to cross over to the enemy's side. If we do so, we should expect to face the power and wrath of God head-on.

It is possible to get so caught up with the counterfeit psychic powers of the occult that we forget Satan's true intent. Unexplainable phenomena can attract us to the occult like a moth to a killing flame. Paul says, "The coming of the lawless one will be in accordance with the work of Satan displayed in all kinds of counterfeit miracles, signs and wonders, and in every sort of evil that deceives those who are perishing" (2 Thessalonians 2:9–10).

But don't let the curiosity of these pseudo-miracles fool you. Satan's purpose in your life is clear. Jesus said that the devil came "only to steal and kill and destroy" (John 10:10). Involvement in the occult will steal our hunger for God, kill our soul, and destroy any hope of an eternity with God. Satan destroys lives, families, faith, reputations, bank accounts, and anything else we hold to be important.

One reason Jesus came to earth was to "destroy the devil's work" (1 John 3:8). When we volunteer for the occult we have joined Satan's forces and find ourselves opposing the work of Christ.

The most amazing thing is not that this brings out God's anger. The most incredible fact is that the Lord, in

159

The Surprising Side of Grace

His great mercy and grace, does not instantly annihilate us but is willing to give us more time to change our ways.

Occult practices are not limited to Bible times. They continue, of course, in our day. Some of those that seem to be flourishing still include:

• Palmistry—interpreting the future from lines on the palm of the hand. Hardly a city doesn't have its Madame Sophia's (or is it Madame Stephanie?) Palm Readings.

• Fortune-Telling—Crystal balls still exist. A neighbor's adult daughter recently consulted such a person and supposedly "discovered" that her father was not the man married to her mother. You can imagine what that did to their family life.

• Channeling—communicating with people from the past, supposedly allowing them to speak through you.

• Excursions into the Psyche—finding missing persons through a soul walk.

• Divining Rods—using a hazel twig to locate hidden objects (usually ones buried in the ground).

• Automatic Writing and Drawing—disengaging the mind to let another force control what you write or draw.

• Telekinesis—moving objects around a room without physically touching them.

• Levitation—raising up of objects (usually tables) by mental and spiritual powers alone.

• Tarot Cards—telling the future by the use of special cards.

• Magic Balls—foretelling future events by using games and objects to make decisions for you.

• Horoscopes—trusting someone's interpretation of astronomical movements (zodiac signs) to direct one's future.

• Voodoo (both black magic and white magic)—calling on evil spirits and demons for personal help or revenge.

• Superstitions—letting black cats, ladders, and unlucky days (Friday the 13th) determine your actions.

• Good Luck Charms—rabbit's feet, horseshoes, four-leaf clovers, lucky numbers—all of which leave your future in trust to unseen and unknowable "fates."

• Psychic Predictors—the ones whose names are splashed across the tabloids, featured on talk shows, and in television commercials who claim the power to foretell future events.

• Satan Worship—outright sacrifice and worship of the evil one.

The list, of course, could go on. The point is that occult activity flourishes, as it has in every age. It was grossly wrong in Jezebel's time, and it still is today. It stirred up God's just anger against Manasseh, and it will do the same for you and me.

Whatever benefits the participants claim from their occult activity is more than negated by the consequences. Satan achieves his end—keeping folks' attention away from God. Biblical guidance is incredibly superior to any help occult sources might provide. God's Word is always true.

And it comes surrounded by God's love, mercy, and grace. God is at work leading us toward eternal life. Satan cares nothing at all for those he dupes. He will use them as long as they can be manipulated to lead others astray, then he will destroy them. Those caught in the occult are willing victims of Satan's annihilation.

Nebuchadnezzar was a Babylonian king who surrounded himself with all the greatest occult advisers in the kingdom. All the wisdom and power of Satan would be given to these men as they gave direction to the potentate of the most powerful, ruthless kingdom on earth. Surely he wouldn't need any more counselors. But four young men captured in Judea are brought to him to add to his staff. These four happen to worship the Lord God, and follow His ways.

How was their advice compared to those occult practitioners? "The king talked with them, and he found none equal to Daniel, Hananiah, Mishael and Azariah; so they entered the king's service. In every matter of wisdom and understanding about which the king questioned them, he found them ten times better than all the magicians and enchanters in his whole kingdom" (Daniel 1:19–20).

Why on earth would anyone take a chance on so-called psychic wisdom, bringing on the just anger of God, when the Bible is so much better?

How does a person know if they are starting to get involved with occult activity? Here are a few guidelines to follow.

Where Do You Turn for Advice?

1. Is this practice condemned outright in the Bible? Some verses need no further explanation. "Do not turn to mediums or seek out spiritists, for you will be defiled by them. I am the LORD your God" (Leviticus 19:31). There's no way to miss the meaning.

2. Does the activity you use for advice call upon some force outside yourself, other than the Holy Spirit? Jesus put it this way, "When he, the Spirit of truth, comes, he will guide you into all truth. He will not speak on his own; he will speak only what he hears, and he will tell you what is yet to come. He will bring glory to me by taking from what is mine and making it known to you" (John 16:13–14). Even the Holy Spirit will not bring us new truth! His role is to help us understand what Jesus has already told us in His Word. The Holy Spirit is the only counselor we will ever need.

3. Are you asked to trust your future to an unknown power? When Madame Sophia reads your palm, under whose authority does she speak? Where does the wisdom come from? Did she make it up? Did she communicate with Satan?

When the 900-number tells you to stay home and not to travel today, where did that advice come from? Was it generated by a computer and a sophisticated answering machine? Or was it a whisper from the devil's lips? Exactly where does all that occult advice come from? No one ever tells us that.

4. In the process of seeking wisdom are you asked to lose control of yourself? It could be a trance (like the young man with the human finger in his pocket), or it could be through hypnosis. What happens when the mind is blanked out? Jesus gives us a hint in Matthew 12:43–45: "When an evil spirit comes out of a man, it goes through arid places seeking rest and does not find it. Then it says, 'I will return to the house I left.' When it arrives, it finds the house unoccupied, swept clean and put in order. Then it goes and takes with it seven other spirits more wicked than itself, and they go in and live there. And the final condition of that man is worse than the first."

5. What would the world be like if everyone used this same process for deciding future actions? What if the entire population read and believed horoscopes? One-twelfth of the world could not leave their houses on any given day. One-twelfth would rush to the mailbox for the "letter of great importance." And only one-twelfth would discover a deeper love relationship with another today. How can one-twelfth of the citizens make a financial kill-ing, if the one-twelfth they were to make a deal with all stay in their room that day? Some systems are based on the premise that most of society will go about their way ignor-ing this wonderful counsel.

6. Does this source provide infallible advice? Has every prediction come true? Has every bit of advice succeeded as promised? Only God knows the future. Satan does not; he can only guess. Because God allows him to exercise certain powers, Satan's average may be slightly higher than your own predictions. The occult tantalizes with claims to "secret information." God has made all things known to all His children in a very public form, the Bible. The real wis-dom for abundant living lies there.

Any psychic predictions that fail to come true prove the seer to be false. "You may say to yourselves, 'How can we know when a message has not been spoken by the LORD?' If what a prophet proclaims in the name of the LORD does not take place or come true, that is a message the LORD has not spoken. That prophet has spoken presumptuously. Do not be afraid of him" (Deuteronomy 18:21–22).

True wisdom from God never errs, and never fails.

As we consider God's just anger against the occult, it's possible that you've discovered that you are now or at one time have been involved in occult activities. How can you avoid the consequences of God's wrath?

How to Just Say No to the Occult

1. Make sure you life has been transferred into the kingdom of God. This means receiving Jesus Christ as Savior and Lord. On the road to the city of Damascus, Jesus explained to Saul of Tarsus what his ministry would be. " 'I am sending you to them to open their eyes and turn them from darkness to light, and from the power of Satan to God, so that they may receive forgiveness of sins and a place among those who are sanctified by faith in me' " (Acts 26:17–18). Later Paul reports "He has rescued us from the dominion of darkness and brought us into the kingdom of the Son he loves, in whom we have redemption, the forgiveness of sins" (Colossians 1:13–14). There is no way to be free from occult bonds if you are still dwelling in darkness.

2. Renounce your occult involvement. Absolutely, completely, unconditionally, thoroughly, unequivocally, definitely, wholly separate yourself immediately from all dealings with the occult. Confess your sin, past or present, to the Lord and to other mature Christians who will hold you to account. Don't whitewash it. Don't think of it as a

minor sin that annoys the Lord. Confess it as a major failure that has stirred God's just anger.

3. Ask for divine deliverance. When teaching the disciples how to pray, Jesus instructed that one of the lines should be, "Deliver us from the evil one" (Matthew 6:13). This assumes that (a) we will need to be delivered, (b) we cannot do it without God's help, and (c) our prayers to Him for assistance will be heard and answered.

4. Immerse yourself in God's Word and in Christian fellowship. Let the pure word of God and accountability to mature believers purge your mind of occult thoughts and your life from occult actions. Paul says, "Though we live in the world, we do not wage war as the world does. The weapons we fight with are not the weapons of the world. On the contrary, they have divine power to demolish strongholds. We demolish arguments and every pretension that sets itself up against the knowledge of God, and we take captive every thought to make it obedient to Christ" (2 Corinthians 10:3–5).

5. Accept God's cleansing with humble joy. We could never break free on our own. Paul said, "I have the desire to do what is good, but I cannot carry it out. For what I do is not the good I want to do; no, the evil I do not what to do—this I keep on doing" (Romans 7:18–19). A few verses later, Paul expresses his joy for God's deliverance, "What a wretched man I am! Who will rescue me from this body of death? Thanks be to God—through Jesus Christ our Lord!" (Romans 7:24–25).

We can be freed from the occult, not because we deserve it, but because of God's great love, mercy, and grace. "How much more, then, will the blood of Christ, who through the eternal Spirit offered Himself unblemished to God, cleanse our consciences from acts that lead to death, so that we may serve the living God!" (Hebrews 9:14).

6. Add one line to your every morning prayer. "Lord, keep me from the evil one." As mentioned above, freedom

from the power and influence of Satan is so central to a believer's life that Jesus made it a part of basic prayer instruction. "Deliver us from the evil one" (Matthew 6:13) should be as much a part of every Christian's prayer as "In Jesus' name, amen."

It should be, of course, a frightening thing to discover that our actions are inciting God's just anger. But that very occult activity offers us dramatic opportunity to experience the cleansing freedom of God's mercy and grace.

Remember it is Satan's purpose to "steal and kill and destroy" (John 10:10). God's intention, even in His expressions of just anger, is found in that same verse, "I have come that they may have life, and have it to the full."

Living the Word

1. Read Isaiah 42:8. If involvement in the occult is to place Satan in the center of your life, how do you think God feels about such activity?

2. Study Isaiah 8:19–20. What is the ultimate test of all wisdom? Instead of seeking the occult, where should we turn?

3. Review and memorize Ephesians 4:27. Is Ephesians written to believers or nonbelievers? What is the grave danger mentioned in this short verse?

4. Now take a look at 2 Timothy 2:25–26. How can we help others who are caught up in occult activities?

5. Finally, read 2 Corinthians 2:11. What does this tell us about our need to be aware of the occult activities around us?

6. You might want to make Psalm 6:4 your prayer:

Turn, O LORD, and deliver me; save me because of your unfailing love.

Chapter 12

The Ultimate Insult

We are a generation of list-makers.

We love lists. Our periodicals are crammed with them. Sports statistics, the stock market, the latest surveys, television schedule, opinion polls, even the jokes on the late-night television talk shows come in lists.

I expect any day now to see the Top Ten List of Top Ten Lists.

Maybe that's why when we look at the subject of God's anger, and we consider the various ways of stirring up His wrath, what we want to know is, which of the various infractions make God most angry? Which is number one on His List of Despicable Deeds?

Well, I don't know the answer to that. I do know that the topics given in the previous ten chapters rightly incite His just anger. And, if all of this has sounded a bit frightening, it should. "It is a dreadful thing to fall into the hands of the living God" (Hebrews 10:31).

But if I had to guess at which sin might provoke God's just anger most severely, I would think it would be whenever we reject the work that Jesus did for our salvation. On the surface it seems unbelievable that anyone, understanding Christ's death on our behalf, would still refuse to call on Jesus as Lord and Savior.

But our world's filled with folks who reject Christ.

The auditorium was packed for the last night of our city-wide evangelistic crusade. Hundreds of workers coming from churches all over town had helped prepare for the meetings. We had prayed, planned, and worked for months to come to this place. At the conclusion of the evangelist's invitation, many responded and came forward to confess their faith. All in all, it was a fruitful effort.

But as I sat on the platform that final Sunday evening I could not help but think of those who had not responded. I looked out and saw Richard, the local chiropractor. He had recently wrecked his third marriage, and behind the façade was a pitifully hurting man. For eight nights he had sat in the fourth row, next to the west wall. Never once did he give any evidence of a commitment to Christ. I kept thinking, "What is he waiting for?"

Then there was Tracy. Three children by three different men. For several months she had lived in a tent on the beach. Now, with government assistance, they had a one-room apartment. She was trapped—she needed the freedom, self-worth, forgiveness, cleansing, and direction that only the Lord could give. For five nights I watched her stand and vigorously sing the final chorus; but never respond to Christ.

Stan and Elizabeth were there every night, too. Dressed impeccably as always, they added proper decorum to audience just as they added a bit of nobility to our regular worship service every week. I knew the depth of their spiritual life was no greater than church attendance. They had been at the top of my prayer list of those I'd wanted to come to Christ during the crusade. The only response I got from them was a hearty handshake, and a "My, it's been an interesting week, Reverend, hasn't it?"

Every night the gospel message had been clearly presented. The opportunity had been given to make a public commitment. But they held back. It saddened me to think that many had come so close to salvation, then held back. They were aware of Christ's work, God's love, and the Holy Spirit's prompting. And I wondered as I watched folks exit

169

the meeting, "How does the Lord feel about those who refuse to accept what Christ has done for them?" And I began to wonder "Is God so strong that His heart won't break?"

One thing I did know. None of this surprises God. He knew it would be this way. Jesus tells the parable of indifferent people in Luke 14:15ff. It begins with a man who decides to host a large dinner party. Following the custom of that day, he sent servants to personally invite the select guests, telling each the day of the party, but not the time. At this point those who knew they had other plans could have graciously declined. Everyone else was expected to attend.

Then the man set out to make all the arrangements for the gala event. The big day came and the decorations were displayed. Lanterns were hung, a choice lamb was slain and roasted, breads were baked. Dried figs, fresh grapes, and pomegranates were selected; the best wine was secured. The seating arrangements were carefully prepared and everything was immaculately clean. The only thing needed was guests. The man sent his servants back to the guests' homes to tell them it was time for the party.

But something shocking, something unheard of, happened. In a terrible insult to Middle-Eastern hospitality, every single invited guest had a last-minute excuse for rejecting the host's hospitality. "They all alike began to make excuses" (Luke 14:18). Some newly purchased property needed to be examined. Some oxen needed to be field-tested. A newly wedded couple were too interested in each other to attend. On and on and on the excuses went.

In today's society of shallow commitments to friendship some might even sound valid. In the culture of that day, they were seen as personal insults. What they were conveying was that they had intended to go to the party only if nothing better came along, and any old excuse would justify their absence.

When the host was told by his servant that absolutely no one was coming to the party, he was furious. "The owner of the house became angry" (14:21). He knew that these were not legitimate excuses. Obviously, they cared little for him and just didn't want to be there.

At that point he sent his servants out again. This time they were urged to "Bring in the poor, the crippled, the blind and the lame" (14:21). But there was more room even after these social outcasts gladly showed up to celebrate. So the host told his servants, "Go out to the roads and country lanes, and make them come in, so that my house will be full. I tell you, not one of those men who were invited will get a taste of my banquet" (14:23–24).

Why did Jesus tell such a story?

The host represents God. Those who refuse His kingdom banquet are those who have rejected Christ, His Son. God is angry with those who have so mistreated His divine invitation.

What Makes God So Irate?

1. To reject Christ is to reject God's wisdom.

The salvation of humanity developed according to a careful and intricate plan. God determined to send His Son to earth as the focal point of that plan from the very beginning. "He was chosen before the creation of the world, but was revealed in these last times for your sake" (1 Peter 1:20).

Jesus understood His part in that plan as He walked the earth. At least three times He warned His followers that the Father's eternal design for their salvation included His own death: "the Son of Man must suffer many things, and be rejected by the elders, chief priests and teachers of the law, and that he must be killed and after three days rise again. He spoke plainly about this" (Mark 8:31–32 and again in Mark 9:31 and Mark 10:33–34).

The crisis of the cross and the miraculous joy of the resurrection were not last-minute detours on a plan gone wrong. They were the central point of God's wisdom and provision for our salvation. How could God ever allow such a thing to happen to His Son? Because it was the only way to bring about our needed salvation.

When we reject Christ after hearing the gospel we are saying it was a stupid and easily discarded plan.

2. To reject Christ is to reject God's love.

The passage is familiar.

Perhaps too familiar. It's lost its shock value. Read it again: "God so loved the world that he gave his one and only Son, that whoever believes in him shall not perish but have eternal life" (John 3:16).

Notice the degree of love shown toward us: the sacrifice of God's only Son. Jesus is like no other. He is the unique expression of everything that is the Father. "He is the image of the invisible God, the firstborn over all creation. For by him all things were created: things in heaven and on earth, visible and invisible, whether thrones or powers or rulers or authorities; all things were created by him and for him. He is before all things, and in him all things hold together" (Colossians 1:15–17).

Out of a deep love, out of mercy without limit, out of abundant grace, God designed a frightfully expensive plan for our salvation. He sent His Son to die for us. There is nothing on the face of this earth that He could have done to prove His love for us in a more dramatic way.

To reject Christ is a slap in God's face and a statement that we intend to get along without His love.

3. To reject Christ is to spurn God Himself.

Some folks act as though the decision to choose or reject Christ is in the same league as to choose whether to live in Tucson or Tampa, Reno or Roanoke, Detroit or Denver. For them it's all a matter of personal preference and choice of lifestyles. According to these people, someone selects his or her automobile, political party, silverware pattern, and religious beliefs with similar forethought and consideration.

But Jesus isn't competing for Entertainer of the Year. We aren't asked to cast our ballot for our favorite religious superstar. Jesus is God.

"In the beginning was the Word, and the Word was with God, and the Word was God" (John 1:1). "He was even calling God his own Father, making himself equal with God" (John 5:18). "I and the Father are one" (John 10:30). "Anyone who has seen me has seen the Father" (John 14:9). "God was pleased to have all his fullness dwell in him" (Colossians 1:19).

When the invited guests in Jesus' parable said they were not coming to the banquet, it was not the servant or messenger that they offended, but the host himself. A person who rejects Christ because he or she doesn't like some Christians, or because a particular church "doesn't meet his or her needs" or because they feel the teaching of the Bible is "too narrow" has not understood the seriousness of his or her behavior.

On a sunny California beach I presented the gospel message to a deeply tanned young man. Then I asked him if he would like to accept Christ. "If you can make God appear right in front of me instantly, then I'll believe," he insisted. "Go ahead," he urged. "See, you can't do it! God didn't appear, and that proves He isn't real."

"Actually," I countered, "it proves God's love and grace. You just blasphemed the Lord Almighty by your demand, and He didn't instantly strike you dead like you deserve. He gave you a little more time. Now is that a God who really loves you, or what?"

"I like my interpretation better," he huffed.

"And I like mine," I insisted. "Yours is based on your own invention, and mine is the clear teaching of the Bible. You aren't rejecting my religion," I cautioned, "you're rejecting God, Himself."

"I don't want to hear about it," he asserted and he grabbed up his beach towel and headed for the parking lot.

Nobody wants to be told they're personally insulting God.

4. To reject Christ means is to reject God's forgiveness.

Divine forgiveness is our only hope. And every one of us knows it. No matter how agnostic or atheistic we might claim to be, none of us wants to receive what we deserve. We hope that our failures are not seen by others, or at least that they're quickly forgotten.

But we can't forget them. Our only hope is to somehow have such actions purged from our past, present, and future. The Bible tells us "If we confess our sins, he is faithful and just and will forgive us our sins and purify us from all unrighteousness" (1 John 1:9).

It is a betrayal of our spirit to reject God's forgiveness. Notice how thoroughly He wants to deal with that sin. "I will forgive their wickedness and will remember their sins no more" (Jeremiah 31:34). It is the chance of a lifetime. It's an opportunity to come to peace with oneself, our own failure, and with eternity.

When we reject Christ we have forfeited all of that.

5. To reject Christ is to reject God's fatherhood.

As people created by God, every human on this earth is entitled to enjoy many of His blessings. "He causes his sun to rise on the evil and the good, and sends rain on the righteous and the unrighteous" (Matthew 5:45). Each one of us is special because we have been created in God's image. "God created man in his own image, in the image of God he created him; male and female he created them" (Genesis 1:27).

But all of that does not mean that we are born "God's children." That position is ours to gain, but it is not our birthright. "To all who received him [Jesus], to those who believed in his name, he gave the right to become children of God" (John 1:12).

Accepting Christ means being adopted into God's family. "How great is the love the Father has lavished on us, that we should be called children of God! And that is what we are!" (1 John 3:1).

God's family members stand in line to inherit a rich legacy. We are granted security against the attacks of the world, the flesh, and the devil. It means we have an eternal home, custom-designed for us. It means we have the power of God dwelling in us so that we can conquer our old sinful nature. It means that we are allowed to experience the fully satisfying joy of fellowship with an almighty Creator whom we are encouraged to call our "Father."

Like a starving orphan who refuses a nice home, so are those who reject the offer to become a part of God's family.

All of this gives us a slight picture of the serious offense of rejecting Christ's sacrifice on our behalf. If that love were trivial, then its rejection would be of little significance.

Accepting God's love for us in Christ means much more than just a warm and sentimental feeling of gratitude. Our experience should include the following:

• We should know beyond all doubt that we have eternal life (1 John 5:11–12).

• We should know that God hears our every prayer (1 John 5:15).

• We should be free from the continual practice of sin (1 John 5:18).

• We should know that Satan cannot harm us (1 John 5:18).

• We should know that Jesus Christ is an intimate friend of ours (1 John 5:13–15).

• We should experience an abiding (continual dwelling) in God and He in us (1 John 4:15).

Rejecting God's love gift of His Son rightfully stirs His anger. And the more we understand His anger, the more we should desire to escape its just consequences. But can any of us know for sure that we've responded properly to the work of Christ for us?

Signs of Having Accepted God's Love

1. We will find it easy to acknowledge our own worthlessness apart from Christ. Paul said "Here is a trustworthy saying that deserves full acceptance: Christ Jesus came into the world to save sinners—of whom I am the worst" (1 Timothy 1:15). This is not the confession of a new convert, fresh from a life of debauchery and rebellion. This is Paul, the old man, at the end of an exemplary life of ministry and service. The years only made him more aware than ever, of God's great love and mercy toward sinful people.

2. We will have a hunger to know Christ at a deeper level, no matter what the personal cost. In Philippians 3:10–11 Paul states, "I want to know Christ and the power of his resurrection and the fellowship of sharing in his sufferings, becoming like him in his death, and so, somehow, to attain to the resurrection from the dead." To those separated from the Lord such a request would seem bizarre. To those who will accept it, Christ offers an attraction that overwhelms caution and pulls us toward greater knowledge of Him.

3. We will be moved to praise when we think of all Jesus has done for us. We often see this kind of response by biblical writers, "Grace and peace to you from God our Father and the Lord Jesus Christ, who gave himself for our sins to rescue us from the present evil age, according to the will of our God and Father, to whom be glory for ever and ever. Amen" (Galatians 1:3–5). Praise is a natural response to the love we feel from God. Once we have accepted Christ we will find our days inexplicably punctuated with praise.

4. We will find ourselves volunteering for good works. We do not labor under a whip. Our actions, after accept-

ing God's love, are not in order to appease a fickle deity. Just the opposite is true. Real faith shows itself in a desire to do good.

Notice the progression in Paul's teaching in Ephesians 2:8–10: "It is by grace you have been saved, through faith—and this not from yourselves, it is the gift of God— not by works, so that no one can boast. For we are God's workmanship, created in Christ Jesus to do good works, which God prepared in advance for us to do."

5. We will find it easy to speak about our allegiance to the Lord. Our relationship with Christ came about by our verbal confession. "If you confess with your mouth, 'Jesus is Lord,' and believe in your heart that God raised him from the dead, you will be saved. For it is with your heart that you believe and are justified, and it is with your mouth that you confess and are saved" (Romans 10:9–10).

When the supreme court of the day demanded that Peter and John quit preaching about Jesus, their response was, "We cannot help speaking about what we have seen and heard" (Acts 4:20). We do not have the capacity to withhold good news. Whether it's the announcement of an engagement, an upcoming birth, a raise at work, or an honor received; we have to talk about it.

Knowing Christ in a personal way is the most incredible good news anyone has ever received.

6. We will find we are no longer handcuffed by our fear of dying. One of the victories brought about by Christ's death was to "free those who all their lives were held in slavery by their fear of death" (Hebrews 2:15).

What does it feel like to have the cloud of death removed from our lives? Listen to Paul. " 'Where, O death, is your victory? Where, O death, is your sting?' The sting of death is sin, and the power of sin is the law. But thanks be to God! He gives us the victory through our Lord Jesus Christ" (1 Corinthians 15:55–57).

7. We will discover a supernatural power available to us that transcends our own human strength. Jesus promised the disciples "You will receive power when the Holy Spirit comes on you; and you will be my witnesses in Jerusalem, and in all Judea and Samaria, and to the ends of the earth" (Acts 1:8).

Paul makes it clear that the Holy Spirit dwells in all believers when he states, "You, however, are controlled not by the sinful nature but by the Spirit, if the Spirit of God lives in you. And if anyone does not have the Spirit of Christ, he does not belong to Christ" (Romans 8:9).

8. We will detect that we have a strong desire to be with the Lord. "I desire to depart and be with Christ, which is better by far . . ." Paul writes in Philippians 1:23. The saints that are catalogued in Hebrews 11 were "longing for a better country—a heavenly one" (Hebrews 11:16). And what was there reward for such a longing? "God is not ashamed to be called their God, for he has prepared a city for them" (Hebrews 11:16).

How do you feel when someone scrimps and saves and buys you a very expensive present? Many of us react by protesting, "I can't accept this. I don't deserve it. You shouldn't spend this much on me. I can't possibly give you anything nearly this nice!"

But often if we take time to look in their eyes and really understand their words, we realize that it is their heart's desire to give us this gift. To reject such a sacrifice would be insulting and perhaps destroy their love and concern for us.

God's gift of His Son is a very expensive present. "The wages of sin is death, but the gift of God is eternal life in Christ Jesus our Lord" (Romans 6:23).

We surely don't deserve it.

We cannot pay Him back.

With humble gratitude we can reach out and clutch it.

Or in stubborn rebellion we can shove it back in His face.

That's the ultimate insult.

It should be no surprise to discover such action awakens His final, ultimate anger.

Living the Word

1. Study the following verses and jot down a word or phrase that indicates how God deals with our sin.

Psalm 32:1–2

Psalm 51:1–2

Isaiah 44:22

Psalm 51:9

Psalm 103:12

Micah 7:18–19

2. Now read aloud Ephesians 1:7; Colossians 1:13–14; and Hebrews 9:22. What do these verses tell us about the basis for God's forgiveness?

3. Review Acts 10:43 and Acts 13:38–39. How do these verses suggest we appropriate God's forgiveness?

4. Knowing that God is holy and just, as well as gracious and loving, what, in your opinion, should be His reaction to those who knowingly reject Christ's death on the cross for their sins?

5. If a friend of yours came and admitted that he or she was afraid of God's wrath but didn't know how to escape it, what three things would you tell that one to do? What is your scriptural support for your advice?

6. You might like to use Psalm 51:10–12 for your prayer:

Create in me a pure heart, O God, and renew a steadfast spirit within me. Do not cast me from your presence or take your Holy Spirit from me. Restore to me the joy of your salvation and grant me a willing spirit, to sustain me.

Chapter 13

The Wrath of the Lamb

The Bible is intricately woven together by dozens of central themes. Part of its majesty comes from the way at least forty different authors living during a span of 1,600 years could weave such a united, cohesive history of God's work in this world. Many of us modern authors can't do that well with a 200-page manuscript that we write by ourselves.

One theme is that of a coming Messiah with vague hints in Genesis 3 and His triumphant victory in the book of Revelation. Then there is the intriguing peek into the spirit world with the fall of Satan, his dominions over the earth, and his prophesied doom. Throughout Scripture we find the topic of God's mighty love and concern for humankind, with its ultimate expression nailed to the cross on Calvary.

But perhaps the most overlooked Bible theme in our present day is that of the coming day of God's anger, called the Day of Wrath.

Universal history is moving in a distinct direction. Life on earth is not static. We are going somewhere. All roads lead to the culmination of God's final fury. We can call this Judgment Day. Or the Day of Reward, or even, the Day of Justice. The New Testament calls it the Day of Wrath. It is foretold in Matthew 3:7 when John the Baptist chided the Pharisees and Sadducees for their phony religious actions. "You brood of vipers! Who warned you to flee from the coming wrath?"

The wrath to come.

God's final anger.

The New Testament closes in Revelation with a graphic portrayal of the enactment of God's anger. It is the birth pangs of a new era and the death knell for an old one. A person has to do some fancy theological sidestepping to ignore the truth about God's wrath. Jesus often warned His followers to be aware of the approaching of that day. Notice the flow of predicted world events that He lists in Matthew 24–25:

• False religious leaders. "Many will come in my name" (24:5).

• Political upheaval. "Wars and rumors of wars" (24:6).

• Natural catastrophes. "Famines and earthquakes in various places" (24:7).

• Severe testings for the faithful. "Persecuted and put to death" (24:9).

• Apostasy in the churches. "Many will turn away from the faith" (24:10).

• Increase in ungodliness. "The love of most will grow cold" (24:12).

• Worldwide evangelization. "Preached in the whole world" (24:14).

• Blasphemy of all that is holy. "The abomination that causes desolation" (24:15).

• Severe tribulations. "Great distress, unequaled from the beginning of the world until now" (24:21).

• The earth-shattering return of the Lord. "The sun will be darkened, and the moon will not give its light; the stars will fall from the sky, and the heavenly bodies will be shaken" (24:29).

• Exaltation of the faithful. "They will gather his elect" (24:31).

• Rejection of foolish unbelievers. "I tell you the truth, I don't know you" (25:12).

• Rewards for the faithful. "Well done, good and faithful servant!" (25:21).

• Banishment, terror, and eternal condemnation for the wicked. "Throw that worthless servant outside, into the darkness, where there will be weeping and gnashing of teeth" (25:30).

In all, it is one of the longest—and certainly the most graphic—sermon of Jesus we have recorded. And it's a detailed description of the coming Day of Wrath.

All the people of the earth will be affected by that day. No amount of economic or political power will help relieve the consequences. "Then the kings of the earth, the princes, the generals, the rich, the mighty, and every slave and every free man hid in caves and among the rocks of the mountains" (Revelation 6:15).

And what were they cowering from? "Hide us from the face of him who sits on the throne and from the wrath of the Lamb" (Revelation 6:16).

The Wrath of the Lamb

Revelation 6 describes that day by using the symbols of four horsemen. The one riding the white horse will conquer, the red one will take peace from the earth, the black one brings famine, and the pale horse brings death.

In Revelation 16, seven angels announce seven last plagues: painful sores, seas smitten, rivers devastated, scorching heat, darkness, widespread destruction, a fierce war against God, and God's final, complete victory over evil. This will be a day when the earth shakes, islands and mountains disappear, cities collapse, and one-hundred-pound hailstones flatten the earth.

The Day of Wrath.

Human limitations hamper the description.

It would seem that every person on the face of the earth should tremble on that day.

But they won't.

Some will actually celebrate it with joy. It is a great day for all who have resisted evil in the face of ridicule, suffering, and death.

"Hallelujah! Salvation and glory and power belong to our God, for true and just are his judgments" (Revelation 19:1–2).

"Praise our God, all you his servants, you who fear him both small and great!" (19:5).

"Hallelujah! For our Lord God Almighty reigns. Let us rejoice and be glad and give him glory! For the wedding of the Lamb has come, and his bride has made herself ready" (19:6–7).

And who is the One to whom the faithful gather in the throne room to direct their praise? Who is the One who instigates the day that is so terrible and so glorious all at the same time?

The King of king and Lord of lords. Jesus, the gentle Savior. Jesus, the lover of children. Jesus, the One who suffered without complaint. This very same Jesus will begin an eternal rule, not only in the hearts and lives of believers, but over all the created universe as well.

Why is this one day so dreaded and yet so eagerly anticipated at the same time? It's because the earth is populated with two kinds of people: those who choose to reject God's truth and those who accept it. It's easy to distinguish which group you belong to.

Characteristics of Those Who Fear the Day of God's Wrath

1. They refuse to believe in God's Son.

"Whoever believes in the Son has eternal life, but whoever rejects the Son will not see life, for God's wrath remains on him" (John 3:36).

2. They reject the limited revelation that all men receive from God in their conscious being.

"The wrath of God is being revealed from heaven against all the godlessness and wickedness of men who suppress the truth by their wickedness, since what may be known about God is plain to them, because God has made it plain to them" (Romans 1:18–19).

3. They stubbornly refuse to admit their sin or to change their ways.

"Because of your stubbornness and your unrepentant heart, you are storing up wrath against yourself for the day of God's wrath, when his righteous judgment will be revealed" (Romans 2:5).

4. They talk about religion in empty theories and deceptive words.

"Let no one deceive you with empty words, for because of such things God's wrath comes on those who are disobedient" (Ephesians 5:6).

5. They are filled with immorality, sensuality, and greed.

"Put to death, therefore, whatever belongs to your earthly nature: sexual immorality, impurity, lust, evil desires and greed, which is idolatry. Because of these, the wrath of God is coming" (Colossians 3:5–6).

6. They do not know God nor respect the claims of His Son.

"He will punish those who do not know God and do not obey the gospel of our Lord Jesus" (2 Thessalonians 1:8).

The Day of Wrath for these will bring eternal separation from God's presence and glory, and the penalty of eternal torment.

"They will be punished with everlasting destruction and shut out from the presence of the Lord and from the majesty of his power on the day he comes to be glorified in his holy people and to be marveled at among all those who have believed" (2 Thessalonians 1:9–10).

Just in case the message isn't clear enough, Revelation 14:10–11 gives more details: "He will be tormented with burning sulfur in the presence of the holy angels and of the Lamb. And the smoke of their torment rises for ever and ever. There is no rest day or night. . . ."

But Scripture also contain the glorious good news that not all will face the final day with fear and trembling. Through no good works of their own, but by God's saving power through Jesus Christ, some will face a different world to come.

At one time we were all headed toward condemnation. "All of us also lived among them at one time, gratifying the cravings of our sinful nature and following its desires and thoughts. Like the rest, we were by nature objects of wrath" (Ephesians 2:3).

But God, in His great mercy and love, provided a plan to deliver us from that just wrath. "For God did not appoint us to suffer wrath but to receive salvation through our Lord Jesus Christ" (1 Thessalonians 5:9). This is made possible by the death of Christ on the cross. "Since we have now been justified by his blood, how much more shall we be saved from God's wrath through him!" (Romans 5:9).

Listen to what awaits those who believe: "But because of his great love for us, God, who is rich in mercy, made us alive with Christ even when we were dead in transgressions—it is by grace you have been saved. And God raised us up with Christ and seated us with him in the heavenly realms in Christ Jesus, in order that in the coming ages he might show the incomparable riches of his grace, expressed in his kindness to us in Christ Jesus" (Ephesians 2:4–7).

All of those who accept Christ as Lord and Savior will find heaven to be a place where "He will wipe every tear from their eyes. There will be no more death or mourning or crying or pain for the old order of things has passed away" (Revelation 21:4).

"Fire-and-brimstone" sermons of a previous era have disappeared in the past fifty years. Many believe to the great benefit of all.

But I wonder, where will people of our generation learn the truth of God's full nature? The harangues of old may have been crudely formed and sometimes insensitively delivered, but they served a vital purpose. No one within shouting distance was fooled into thinking everyone would end up in heaven. Even if they rejected the message, they knew they would someday face the full brunt of God's fury.

The message is biblical.

Critical.

Urgent.

Every person on this globe deserves to hear plainly, at least once as they pass through this life, about God's wrath.

Having carefully considered the surprising side of grace and learned to better appreciate God's loving, just anger, what should we do now?

If you've never accepted Jesus Christ as Lord and Savior, now is the time. The anger of God now, the Day of Wrath to come, and the eternal punishment of hell need not be a part of your life. The information in this book is not meant to scare you into an insincere decision. It is a clear, straight-up warning of what God has revealed about Himself, and about the future. To fail to convey such knowledge to you would be a horrible omission and gross spiritual neglect.

But how about those of us who do believe? The topic of God's anger is not merely a theological discussion reserved for idle Sunday afternoons. There are at least five things such a study should motivate us to do.

1. We should acknowledge that just anger is an absolute, necessary attribute of God's personality.

We believe that justice takes place when people get exactly what they deserve. No more. No less. God's anger, both now and in the Day of Wrath, is His confirmation that justice will be satisfied.

187

God's anger is His determined action to punish sin. He is always fair. Every sin has a price. There are no discount sales on the way to the Pearly Gates.

There would be no justice, now or in the world to come, in a world ruled by an angerless God.

2. We must stand in reverential awe of God's power.

We must never forget who we are dealing with. You and I stand as merely one of many billions who have walked this planet. We are in a second-rate solar system in a galaxy that has millions of planets. Surrounding us, we are told, are innumerable other galaxies.

Yet, too often, we dare to blithely disobey God. The God who merely had to speak the word and those worlds were created. It is Jesus whom many take lightly, who holds this creation together (Colossians 1:17). We blindly play games of chance with One who knows our every thought before we utter it. We cannot hide from Him who knows every wart and blemish on our spirits and souls.

In spite of all this, God loves us deeply. Even as the crushing weight of God's just anger continues to roll closer with every year, He keeps calling us to life. When we look closely at His just anger we should experience an overwhelming feeling of gratefulness.

3. We should offer God more praise for His deliverance.

Two divergent dramas dominate the book of Revelation. On earth, the final Tribulation will wreak plagues and havoc on those who choose to reject God's love.

In heaven, mighty throngs will sing stirring waves of praise choruses to the Lord.

"Holy, holy, holy is the Lord God Almighty, who was, and is, and is to come" (Revelation 4:8).

"Worthy is the Lamb, who was slain, to receive power and wealth and wisdom and strength and honor and glory and praise!" (Revelation 5:12).

"Amen! Praise and glory and wisdom and thanks and honor and power and strength be to our God for ever and ever. Amen!" (Revelation 7:12).

"We give thanks to you, Lord God Almighty, the One who is and who was, because you have taken your great power and have begun to reign. The nations were angry; and your wrath has come. The time has come for judging the dead, and for rewarding your servants the prophets and your saints and those who reverence your name, both small and great—and for destroying those who destroy the earth" (Revelation 11:17–18).

These are the songs of the soaring joy of justice fulfilled. It is the gratitude and relief of escape. Believers in Christ literally risk their lives on the certain hope of eternity based on the just plan of God. When that plan finally is carried to completion, rejoicing is in order.

We can begin that heavenly number with our earthly choruses. We can overflow with praise even now. God holds us tight and secure from the fury of His wrath, which our sinful nature deserves.

Hallelujah!

4. We should be encouraged to rededicate our lives to God's service.

Are there any things you've felt that you just had to do in response to another? What about sending a thank-you note to a loved one for a gift? Or telling your mate you love him or her? Or smiling when someone surprises you with a compliment? What about shaking hands with a neighbor who offers friendship?

Some situations demand a response.

A second-grade girl slipped me a note before church. In her charming elementary-school style she wrote how much I meant to her as a pastor. Now, theoretically it's possible that I could have tossed this sentiment aside as if it were no big deal. But the truth is, I found myself wiping my eyes and stammering appreciation for an eight-year-old's kind affirmation. It was the type of action that demanded an active response.

So it is with God's love, mercy, and grace. If I felt compelled to respond to a young girl, how much more to the love offered to me from the heavenly Father? His work on our behalf should compel me to give myself to Him.

"Lord, what can I say? I am speechless because I realize how much I don't deserve to be accepted into Your presence. Yet, here I am, Lord. Like a child not knowing how to express what I'm feeling, I stammer—Lord, excuse me, but I just wanted to say—thanks! And one more thing: Is there anything I can do for You?"

That's what rededication is all about.

5. We should renew our enthusiasm to reach the lost.

True knowledge of God's anger should make evangelists out of us all. Everyone will face that wrath sooner or later. That means the native in the bush, the millions in inland Asia, the folks in the inner-cities, and the isolated cowboy who still rides the range. It means we need to talk about the Jesus who can deliver us from the consequence of God's just wrath to Uncle Jake, little Suzanne, and even Crazy Eddie at work.

We are told "Be merciful to those who doubt: snatch others from the fire and save them; to others show mercy, mixed with fear—hating even the clothing stained by corrupted flesh" (Jude 22–23).

Dwelling on God's anger doesn't have to be the focus of every thought, message, or testimony, but it should remain at the core of our motivation. We must demonstrate that we really do care about the eternal destiny of those around us.

One of my favorite spots to view the majesty of God's creation is Yosemite National Park in California. I am especially attracted to Glacier Point. From the tops of those cliffs I have an unobstructed view of such wonders as Half Dome, Nevada Falls, and the upper glacier valleys. From the edge of the cliff I can look straight down 3,000 feet to the Yosemite Valley floor.

But all along the edge of that sheer granite is a very practical device, a simple metal guardrail. It has an obvious purpose. One step beyond that rail could be fatal. There is no more exhilarating feeling than to stand at the rail's edge and drink in the vastness of the Sierra Nevada mountains. I don't feel in the least restricted or repressed. If I think of the rail at all, it is only to remember that someone cares about my safety.

To respect God's anger is to show consideration for the guardrail of our souls and spirits. We can know when we have stepped too close to the edge of eternal destruction. That fence of God's anger marks the boundaries of His love and mercy and grace.

Hanging on the guardrail at Glacier Point is a sign that reads "Stay Behind the Rails." Once I leaned over as far as I could to see what was on the back of that sign. It was blank. There was no reason to put a message on the backside. Once you were there, it would be too late. You would have begun your fatal descent.

The warning about God's anger needs to be given now. We cannot wait until Judgment Day and then say to others, "Oh, didn't I tell you about this?"

It is a positive message we have to proclaim because there is still time to heed the warning. No one need to experience God's anger. Jesus provides us with forgiveness and deliverance from the just wrath to come.

Even though examining the nature of God's anger is not a popular topic, it remains a critical ingredient. Without that knowledge our view of Him, of life, of eternity, will be stunted.

Every true spiritual pilgrimage must include knowledge of God's righteous, loving anger. Then, and only then, will we be able to comprehend such words as sin, repentance, blasphemy, justice, and hell.

The Surprising Side of Grace

And only with a proper view of God's anger can we truly appreciate the awe-inspiring sweetness of such terms as mercy, grace, forgiveness, and love.

Living the Word

1. Study Revelation 19:11–16. Who is it describing? What is about to take place? Is this a cause of fear or rejoicing?

2. Meditate again on Romans 3:23 and Romans 6:23. If God were to decide today to give you exactly what you deserved, what should He do?

3. When was the last time you talked to a nonbeliever about the wrath of God? Where did the conversation lead? How would you now do it differently?

4. Complete the following: When I think seriously about God's just anger I feel _____ and it makes me want to _____.
Were your answers biblical?

5. Name three people you know who really need to hear clearly these words about God's anger:
   a.
   b.
   c.
What can you do to help them explore this topic without beating them over the head with it?

6. You might like to make Psalm 106:47 your prayer:

Save us, O LORD our God, and gather us from the nations, that we may give thanks to your holy name and glory in your praise.